LIVING THROUGH THE CYCLE

MY PAIN IS REAL

Living through the Cycle:

My Pain is REAL!

By:

Teri Rushawn Rogers

Table of Contents

INTRODUCTION

Breaking Stigmas, Building Bridges: Our Voices, Our Stories, Our Strength

In a world that often prioritizes surface appearances over the complex array of human experience, this book stands as a beacon of hope and understanding. It has been thoughtfully assembled to elevate awareness, nurture education, and galvanize community support around the complicated and multifaceted issue of women's mental health. Our spotlight is cast upon culturally responsive care, a crucial element often overlooked in traditional mental health discourse, as well as highlighting under recognized conditions like Premenstrual Dysphoric Disorder (PMDD) that disproportionately impact marginalized groups.

First and foremost, mental health is a universal human right.

It is essential for achieving a fulfilling life where individuals can pursue their passions, adopt connections, and embody their true selves. However, the stark reality is that stigma and systemic barriers create formidable obstacles that disproportionately affect minorities. This distortion leads to an environment where those who most need support may feel isolated or ashamed to seek help, perpetuating a cycle of silence and suffering.

By addressing these stigmas head on, we can take significant strides toward an inclusive understanding of mental health that uplifts everyone.

Next, it's vital to shed light on Premenstrual Dysphoric Disorder (PMDD), a serious yet often un derecognized condition that wreaks havoc on the lives of those it affects. PMDD goes beyond com mon menstrual symptoms, leading to debilitating emotional and physical distress. Its symptoms can mimic or exacerbate other mental health disorders, compounding the challenges for those in communities of color who may already be navigating a maze of societal pressures and a lack of access to proper care.

Raising awareness around PMDD is not just about recognizing a specific diagnosis; it's about validating the experiences of countless women who feel unheard and invisible in their struggles. Healing and wellness thrive in environments where communities root for one another, building bridges across cultural divides, generational gaps, and diverse lived experiences. When we share our stories, we sow seeds of understanding and empathy, enabling us to demolish the misconceptions that prolong isolation. Each narrative shared is a thread woven into a collective fabric that fosters resilience, amplifying the strength found in unity and solidarity.

Lastly, it is crucial to recognize the power of personal stories as they serve as vital vehicles for connection, education, and healing. They lay bare the particulars of mental health experiences, inviting listeners to walk alongside the storyteller, to witness their journey, and to learn from their challenges and triumphs. Personal stories transform abstract concepts into tangible realities, revealing the profound impact that empathy and shared experience can have in breaking down barriers and dismantling stigma. By embracing our narratives, we empower ourselves and others, cultivating a community that not only understands but active ly supports one another in the quest for mental wellness.

In conclusion, this book is more than evidence-based research; it is a call to action, A call to recognize our inherent rights to mental health, an invitation to acknowledge and understand conditions like PMDD, and an encouragement to weave stronger community ties that embrace diversity and shared resilience. As we embark on this journey together, let us be reminded that at our voices are powerful, our stories matter, and our collective strength can truly change the landscape of women's mental health for generations to come.

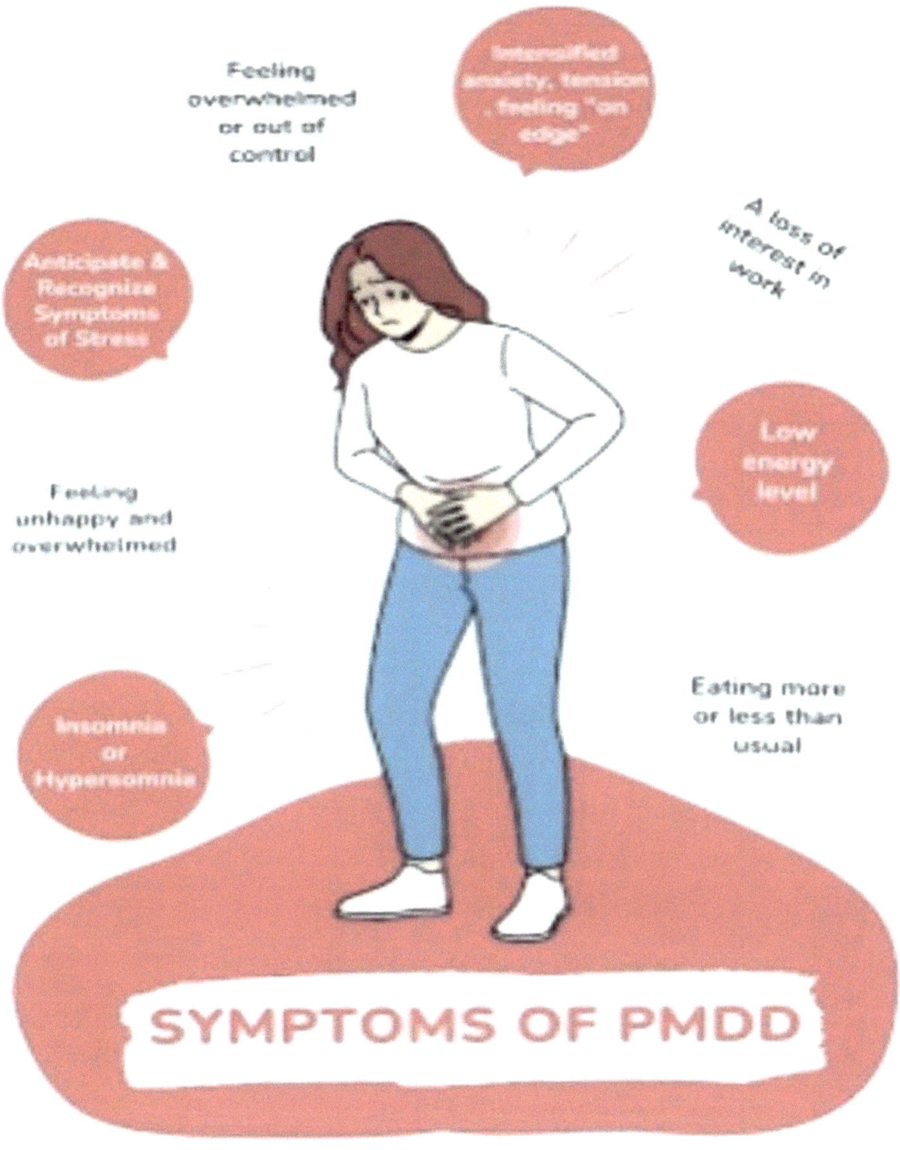
Feeling overwhelmed or out of control
Intensified anxiety, tension, feeling "on edge"
Anticipate & Recognize Symptoms of Stress
A loss of interest in work
Low energy level
Feeling unhappy and overwhelmed
Eating more or less than usual
Insomnia or Hypersomnia
SYMPTOMS OF PMDD

My Story

Living Through the Cycle: My PAIN is REAL

For decades, my voice was silenced beneath layers of misunderstanding. I was gaslit by professionals, dismissed by family, and misunderstood by those I loved most. Each failed relationship left me questioning my worth, never realizing that part of the foundation was built on my codependency and an undiagnosed condition that was ruling my body and mind.

It wasn't until my late thirties that I finally discovered the truth: Premenstrual Dysphoric Disorder (PMDD).

The Weight of Misdiagnosis

In the documentary Game Girls, there's a pivotal moment with a male doctor. He attempted to evaluate me, but when I described my symptoms, he could not recognize PMDD. Instead, his interpretation leaned toward "bipolar disorder," the default diagnosis for women presenting with mood instability. That misstep wasn't unique—it is the reality for millions of women worldwide. PMDD remains invisible in most training manuals, leaving clinicians unprepared to identify it. The urgency is clear: PMDD must be included in mental health treatment plans and clinician training to ensure proper diagnosis and care.

Misdiagnosis has devastating consequences. Substance use disorder, legal entanglements, and destructive coping mechanisms in my life were not born out of carelessness but desperation. I was self-medicating the unbearable symptoms of a hormonal imbalance that no one could name.

A Cultural Reflection

A childhood memory still lingers—a scene from the movie I'm Gonna Get You Sucka. Dawn Lewis' character begged for time off work due to severe cramps. Later, when attacked, she transformed, shouting, "I HAVE CRAMPS!" as she terrified her assailant. For me, that moment captured the raw truth of PMDD. A terrifying, powerful, misunderstood force—dismissed as a joke.

That dismissal mirrored my own lived reality. For years, PMDD was treated as "just PMS." But PMDD is not PMS. It is a disabling, cyclical disorder that disrupts families, workplaces, and lives. That's why I insisted on writing about PMDD in the Workplace—because women with this diagnosis are protected under the Americans with Disabilities Act (ADA). Employers who fail to honor accommodations—such as time off during symptomatic phases—risk violating federal law. Recognition is not just medical; it is legal.

Finding Community, Finding Truth

When I discovered PMDD support groups on Facebook, I finally realized I wasn't alone. These women understood the despair of the luteal phase and the relief that followed. We shared symptom trackers, survival tips, and validation that science had failed to give us.

Even then, solutions remained scarce. When prescribed Lexapro, I spiraled toward suicide—a chilling reminder that the wrong treatment can be more dangerous than the disease itself. I refused to sacrifice my life for a prescription pad's guesswork. Since then, my survival has depended on cycle tracking—charting moods, behaviors, and physical changes, day by day, week by week, year after year.

But without access to specialized behavioral health care, my fight continues to be uphill.

Why This Book Exists

This book was born from necessity—my way of breaking the silence and demanding recognition. Living Through the Cycle: My PAIN is REAL is not just my story; it is a call to action.

- To expand research.
- To equip clinicians with the knowledge to distinguish PMDD from bipolar disorder.

- To protect women in the workplace through ADA recognition.
- To provide real support for those who feel alone, abandoned, or misdiagnosed.

PMDD is not just my battle; it is a global crisis disguised as individual suffering. My pain is real. And so is my determination to turn it into power—for myself, and for every woman still trapped in silence.

PMDD (Premenstrual Dysphoric Disorder)

PMDD (Premenstrual Dysphoric Disorder) is a real, hormone-related mood disorder that requires compassion, clinical care, and understanding.

Important Facts for Providers, Family, and Community:

- PMDD is recognized in the DSM-5
- It affects 3–8% of menstruating individuals
- It is not PMS
- It is not "just emotional"
- It is not imaginary

What I need from you:

- To believe me
- To support me
- To respect my boundaries
- To help me find care, not shame

Learn more: BreakingStigmas.org or IAPMD.org.

Define the Harm Clearly when community members (family, educators, and clinicians) **dismiss PMDD** as "just PMS" or imply it's all in someone's head, that's a form of **medical gaslighting**.

Name it:

"When you invalidate someone's experience by calling it dramatic, hormonal, or 'not real,' that's a form of gaslighting. It causes harm, delays treatment, and isolates the person."

Use **real language** but stay rooted in **facts and compassion**.

Bring Education to the Center

People often dismiss what they don't understand. Normalize education as a tool—not a confrontation.

The heart of understanding PMDD compassionately. Here's a comprehensive explanation that blends the **hormonal science** with the **social and environmental realities**:

PMDD: Hormonal, Not a Choice

1. PMDD is Hormonal and Out of One's Control

- PMDD is triggered by **normal hormonal fluctuations** in estrogen and progesterone after ovulation (the luteal phase).
- People with PMDD are not producing "too much" or "too little" hormone — their brains simply have an **abnormal sensitivity** to these hormonal changes.
- This leads to severe mood symptoms (depression, rage, anxiety, hopelessness), physical pain, and cognitive difficulties.
- The suffering is not a reflection of "weakness" or "overreaction" — it is a **biological reaction** outside of conscious control.

2. Environmental & Lifestyle Factors that Worsen Hormonal Sensitivity

Hormones don't act in isolation. Stress, environment, and social conditions can make symptoms worse:

- **Chronic Stress (financial, housing, caregiving):** Prolonged stress raises cortisol, which destabilizes estrogen/progesterone balance and intensifies PMDD symptoms.

- **Poor Sleep & Irregular Routines:** Disrupt circadian rhythms and hormone regulation.
- **Nutrition & Toxins:** Highly processed foods, endocrine disruptors, and lack of key nutrients (B vitamins, magnesium, vitamin D) worsen hormonal sensitivity.
- **Lack of Support Systems:** Without understanding from family, employers, or healthcare providers, stress builds — magnifying hormone-triggered symptoms.

3. Financial Stress & Lack of Awareness

- **Financial strain** limits access to therapy, specialists, or even time off during severe symptom days.
- Many can't afford consistent treatment, which worsens the hormonal/mental health cycle.
- **Lack of awareness** — even among doctors — delays diagnosis for an average of **8–12 years**, leaving people to suffer untreated.

4. Gaslighting & Minimization

- People with PMDD are often **dismissed as moody, dramatic, or "just PMS-ing."**
- This gaslighting doesn't only happen in medical offices — it often occurs in **day-to-day conversations:**
    - A partner saying: "Oh, you're just hormonal again."
    - Friends joking: "She's on her period, ignore her."
- Even when said "playfully," these comments **invalidate real suffering** and deepen shame, isolation, and self-doubt.
- Over time, this can damage trust in relationships and make individuals

less likely to seek help.

5. The Double Burden

- PMDD itself is disabling.
- On top of that, **social stigma, lack of structural support, financial barriers, and casual dismissal** create an added layer of harm.
- This double burden worsens the risk of depression, relationship breakdowns, job loss, and suicidal thinking.

PMDD is not a matter of "willpower" or "attitude" — it's a **hormone-driven disorder** that's worsened by environmental stress, lack of awareness, and dismissive social responses.

- Just as someone with diabetes can't "control" insulin response, someone with PMDD cannot "control" their brain's hormone sensitivity.
- Compassion, support, and structural accommodations are essential to reducing the suffering caused not just by hormones, but by the world's response to them.

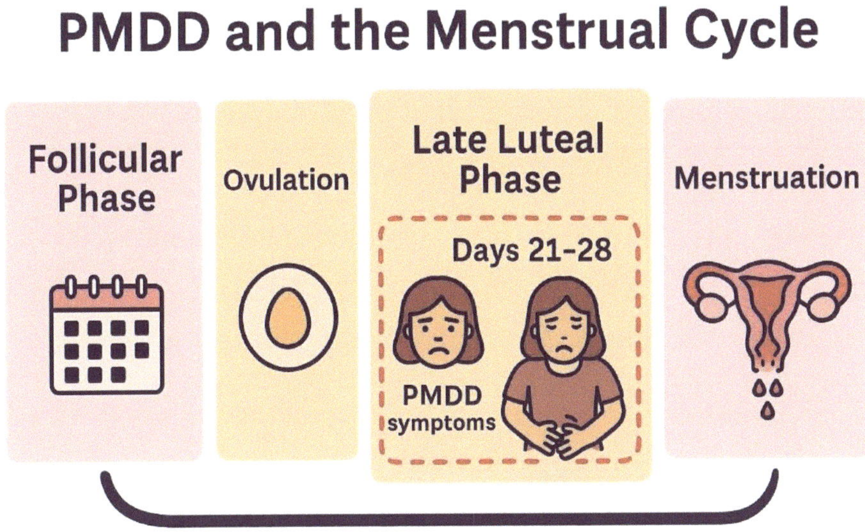
PMDD and the Menstrual Cycle
Follicular Phase
Ovulation
Late Luteal Phase
Days 21-28
PMDD symptoms
Menstruation

Challenge Gaslighting with Cultural Reframing

Communities of color often **survive through strength**, and that strength can sometimes suppress empathy.

Holding a community accountable when they attempt to **gaslight or dismiss a diagnosis like PMDD** (or any mental health condition) requires a **balance of education, advocacy, boundary-setting, and cultural sensitivity**. You're working to **shift deeply rooted narratives**—often passed down through generations or reinforced by systems that historically have ignored or pathologized marginalized people.

Here's how you can approach it effectively:

By asking Questions;

- What is PMDD? (Symptoms, diagnosis, and the difference from PMS)
- How it affects mood, relationships, and daily functioning
- Why women of color are often ignored or misdiagnosed
- The emotional toll of not being believed by providers
- What is Gaslighting?

Gaslighting

The term **"gaslight"** (or "gaslighting") refers to a form of psychological manipulation in which someone tries to make another person doubt their own perceptions, memories, or sanity. It's often used in abusive relationships—romantic, familial, professional, or otherwise—where the gaslighter seeks to gain control or avoid accountability.

Origins:

The term originates from the 1938 play Gas Light (and its subsequent film adaptations), where a husband manipulates his wife into thinking she's losing her mind by dimming the gas lights and then denying that the lighting has changed when she notices.

Examples of Gaslighting:

- **Denial:** "That never happened. You're imagining things."
- **Trivializing feelings:** "You're overreacting. It's not that big a deal."

- **Withholding information:** "I don't know what you're talking about," when they do.
- **Shifting blame:** "You're the one who made me do that."

Signs You Might Be Experiencing Gaslighting:

- Constantly second-guessing yourself
- Feeling confused or "crazy"
- Apologizing often
- Making excuses for someone's behavior
- Feeling like you can't do anything right

Why It Matters:

Gaslighting can have serious effects on mental health, including anxiety, depression, and a loss of confidence or sense of self. Recognizing it is a key step toward setting boundaries or seeking support.

Gaslighting is extremely harmful, especially when layered on top of conditions like **PMDD, PTSD, or disability**. Here's a detailed breakdown of the **detriments and harms of gaslighting**:

The Harm of Gaslighting

1. Psychological Harm

- **Self-doubt & confusion:** Victims start questioning their own memory, judgment, and perception of reality.
- **Erosion of confidence:** Constantly being told they are "too sensitive," "imagining things," or "overreacting" chips away at self-esteem.
- **Cognitive dissonance:** Being told their reality is "wrong" creates an

internal conflict that feels destabilizing and exhausting.

- **Increased anxiety & depression:** Gaslighting is strongly linked to higher rates of **depressive episodes, panic attacks, and even suicidal ideation.**

2. Emotional Harm

- **Shame & guilt:** Victims internalize the belief that they are flawed or defective.
- **Isolation:** Because they are told others won't believe them, victims often withdraw from friends, family, or support systems.
- **Hopelessness:** Over time, gaslighting can make people feel trapped, powerless, and convinced no one will understand them.

3. Relational & Social Harm

- **Erosion of trust:** Both trust in oneself and in others deteriorates.
- **Dependency:** Gaslighting makes the victim more reliant on the abuser for a sense of "reality."
- **Social silencing:** When communities, workplaces, or systems gaslight (e.g., dismissing women's pain as "normal PMS"), entire groups are disempowered and stigmatized.

4. Physical Harm

- **Chronic stress response:** Constant invalidation activates the **fight-flight-freeze system**, leading to physical symptoms (headaches, high blood pressure, muscle tension, GI issues).
- **Sleep disruption:** Hypervigilance and racing thoughts interfere with rest, which worsens health and emotional regulation.
- **Health neglect:** Gaslit individuals may delay care, thinking they're

"exaggerating" symptoms — dangerous for conditions like PMDD, autoimmune disease, or trauma recovery.

5. Long-Term Harm

- **Trauma bonding:** Victims may stay connected to harmful people/institutions because their sense of self has been dismantled.
- **Complex PTSD:** Prolonged exposure to gaslighting can cause trauma symptoms — flashbacks, emotional numbing, hypervigilance.
- **Cycle of silence:** Survivors may fear speaking up again in future relationships, workplaces, or healthcare settings, reinforcing systemic oppression.

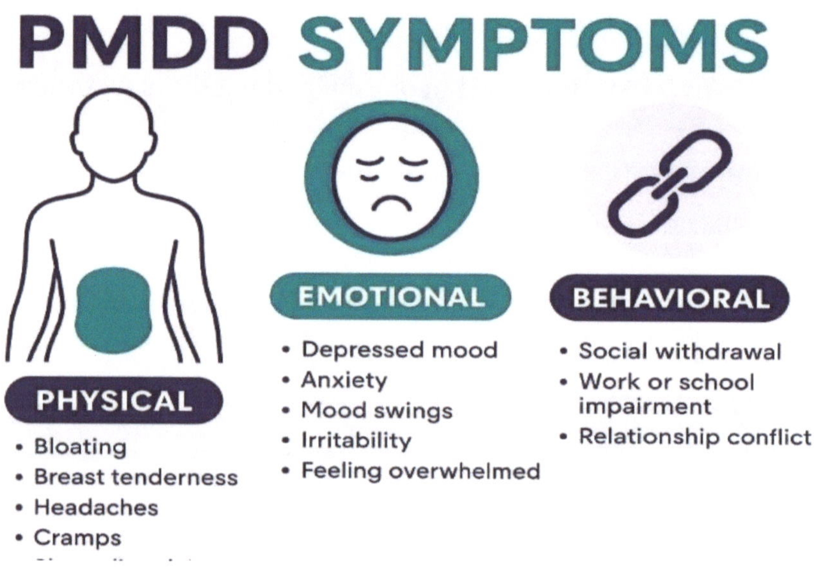

PMDD & Medical Gaslighting

For people with **PMDD**, gaslighting is especially dangerous:

- **Medical dismissal:** Many are told it's "just PMS" or "all in your head," delaying diagnosis for **8–12 years on average.**

- **Cultural bias:** In BIPOC communities, gaslighting combines with racism and sexism, leading to even higher rates of neglect.
- **Suicide risk:** When life-threatening symptoms are minimized, patients lose hope, and safety planning becomes harder.

Gaslighting isn't just manipulation — it's **psychological abuse** that can:

- Undermine reality, safety, and trust.
- Cause long-term trauma and even physical illness.
- Increase risks of **self-harm and suicide** in vulnerable groups (like PMDD patients).

PMDD 101

What PMDD is (vs PMS)

Here's a clear breakdown of **PMDD vs PMS**:

PMS (Premenstrual Syndrome)

- **What it is:** A set of physical and emotional symptoms that occur in the luteal phase of the menstrual cycle (about 1–2 weeks before menstruation).
- **Symptoms:** Bloating, breast tenderness, headaches, mild mood changes (irritability, sadness, anxiety), food cravings, fatigue.
- **Severity:** Generally mild to moderate, and symptoms usually don't interfere heavily with daily functioning.
- **Duration:** Symptoms typically resolve with the start of menstruation or shortly after.

PMDD (Premenstrual Dysphoric Disorder)

"Premenstrual dysphoric disorder is characterized by the presence of mood symptoms (e.g. mood lability, irritability, dysphoria, anxiety symptoms) and other symptoms (e.g. decreased interest in activities, difficulty concentrating, lethargy, marked change in appetite, hypersomnia or insomnia, feeling overwhelmed or out of control, breast tenderness or swelling, joint or muscle pain, a sensation of bloating, or weight gain) that begin sometime following ovulation and remit within a few days of the onset of menses.

These symptoms recur in most menstrual cycles and are associated with significant distress or interference with personal, family, social, educational, occupational, or other important areas of functioning."

- **What it is:** A **severe form of PMS** recognized as a medical and psychiatric disorder (listed in the DSM-5).
- **Symptoms:** All PMS symptoms **plus extreme mood disturbances** such as:
    - Severe depression or hopelessness
        - Intense anxiety or tension
        - Sudden mood swings
    - Irritability or anger that affects relationships
    - Difficulty concentrating
        - Feeling overwhelmed or out of control
        - Physical symptoms (similar to PMS but often more intense)
- **Severity:** Much more severe than PMS—symptoms are **debilitating** and can interfere with work, school, relationships, and overall quality of life. In some cases, PMDD can lead to suicidal thoughts.
- **Duration:** Symptoms occur in the luteal phase (7–14 days before menstruation) and usually improve within a few days after menstruation starts.

Key Differences

Feature	**PMS**	**PMDD**
Recognition	Common but not classified as a mental disorder	Official psychiatric diagnosis (DSM-5)
Severity	Mild–moderate	Severe, life-disrupting
Emotional Symptoms	Mild mood swings, irritability	Extreme mood changes, depression, anxiety, rage
Impact on Daily Life	Generally manageable	Causes significant impairment in work, school, and relationships

To sum things up:

- **PMS = bothersome but manageable • PMDD = severe, disabling, and psychiatric-level condition requiring medical attention**

Below is an outline of **diagnosis and treatment options** side by side, so you can see how doctors approach PMS versus PMDD.

Aspect	**PMS**	**PMDD**
Criteria	Symptoms recurring DSM-5 diagnosis: phase (1– including **1 or more mood-**	At least **5 symptoms**, during the luteal

	related	
	2 weeks before period), but **symptoms** (depression, anxiety, irritability, or not severe mood swings)	
Symptom Tracking	Often based on self-report symptoms are cyclic and severe)	Requires **daily ratings for ≥2 cycles** (to confirm
Impact on Life	Mild to moderate symptoms do not severely daily life	Symptoms **disrupt work, relationships, and functioning impair**
Associated Risks	Usually, there is no long- term mental health risk	Higher risk of **suicidal thoughts/behavior** and comorbid conditions (depression, anxiety, PTSD)

Treatment Approaches

Category	**PMS**	**PMDD**
Lifestyle & Self-Care	Exercise, stress reduction, good sleep, limiting	Same as PMS, but often **not sufficient alone**

Dietary Supplements	caffeine/salt/alcohol Calcium, magnesium, vitamin B6, omega-3 fatty acids sometimes help NSAIDs (ibuprofen, naproxen) for cramps, bloating, headaches	May help as supportive therapy, but **not enough on their own**
Over-the-Counter (OTC)	Some birth control pills to regulate the cycle and lessen PMS	Can help physical symptoms, but **not mood** symptoms
Hormonal Options	Usually not needed	Hormonal treatments are more targeted: oral contraceptives (esp. drospirenone-containing), GnRH agonists (suppress ovulation) **SSRIs (antidepressants) are first-line treatment** — taken daily or only during the luteal phase. It can significantly reduce symptoms.
Psychiatric Medication	Support groups or stress management	**Cognitive Behavioral Therapy (CBT)** helps manage mood and coping

Therapy	Rarely required as a last resort.	In severe, resistant cases, surgical oophorectomy (removal of ovaries) is **Options** considered

Advanced

- **PMS**: Managed with lifestyle changes, self-care, and sometimes mild medication.
- **PMDD**: Requires **medical diagnosis and treatment** — especially antidepressants, hormone therapy, or both.
- Physical, emotional, and behavioral symptoms

Here's a **detailed breakdown of the physical, emotional, and behavioral symptoms of PMDD** (Premenstrual Dysphoric Disorder).

PMDD Symptoms

1. Emotional / Psychological Symptoms

These are the **core and most disabling** features of PMDD, often more intense than PMS:

- **Depressed mood**: deep sadness, hopelessness, or feelings of worthlessness.
- **Anxiety and tension**: feeling "on edge," keyed up, or excessively worried.
- **Mood swings**: rapid shifts from sadness to irritability or anger; heightened sensitivity to rejection.
- **Irritability/anger**: intense frustration or conflict with others, disproportionate to the situation.
- **Decreased interest**: loss of motivation or withdrawal from usual activities (work, hobbies, relationships).
- **Emotional overwhelm**: feeling unable to cope, "out of control," or emotionally flooded.
- **Cognitive difficulties**: poor concentration, forgetfulness, or "brain fog."
- **Suicidal thoughts**: in severe cases, recurrent thoughts of death, self-harm, or suicide.

2. Physical Symptoms

These overlap with PMS but are usually **more severe and persistent** in PMDD:

- **Bloating and water retention**
    - **Breast tenderness or swelling**

- **Headaches or migraines**
- **Joint or muscle pain**
- **Cramps and pelvic pain** (sometimes severe)

- **Gastrointestinal upset** (constipation, diarrhea, nausea)
- **Changes in appetite**: cravings (esp. for sweets, carbs, or salty foods) or reduced appetite
- **Sleep disturbances**: insomnia, restless sleep, or hypersomnia (sleeping too much)
- **Fatigue and low energy**: extreme tiredness, sluggishness, or exhaustion even after rest
- **Hot flashes or night sweats** (in some cases)
  - **Dizziness or lightheadedness**

3. Behavioral / Social Symptoms

These result from the combination of emotional and physical distress:

- **Social withdrawal**: avoiding friends, family, or group activities
- **Work or school impairment**: difficulty focusing, reduced productivity, absenteeism
- **Relationship conflict**: increased arguments, sensitivity, or inability to tolerate stress in relationships
- **Loss of interest in sex** (libido changes)
- **Increased substance use**: some may turn to alcohol, smoking, or overeating for relief

- **Impulsive or risky behavior** during episodes of emotional dysregulation

Summary

- **PMS = discomfort**

- **PMDD = disabling disorder**: The emotional/behavioral symptoms (hopelessness, severe irritability, suicidal ideation) are what make PMDD distinct and far more serious than PMS.

- Symptoms appear in the **luteal phase** (1–2 weeks before menstruation) and **improve shortly after bleeding starts**, making the pattern cyclical and predictable.

- When it shows up (late luteal phase)

Let's look at **when PMDD symptoms show up** in the menstrual cycle:

Timing of PMDD Symptoms

- **Phase:** Symptoms appear in the **late luteal phase** of the menstrual cycle.

- **When this is:** Roughly the **7–14 days before menstruation begins** (after ovulation, before bleeding starts).

- **Peak:** Symptoms are usually **most intense in the final 3–5 days** before the period.

- **Relief:** Symptoms generally **improve within a few days after menstruation begins** and are absent during the **follicular phase** (the first half of the cycle, right after the period ends until ovulation).

- **Cycle pattern:** PMDD symptoms repeat with each cycle, making them **predictable and cyclical.**

Cycle Breakdown

1. Follicular Phase (Day 1–14):

Starts with menstruation. Hormones (estrogen and progesterone) are lower, then estrogen rises—no **PMDD symptoms.**

2. Ovulation (around Day 14 in a 28-day cycle):

The egg is released. Some individuals may experience temporary mid-cycle changes, but PMDD does not manifest in this way.

3. Luteal Phase (Day 15–28):

Progesterone rises after ovulation. In PMDD, the **late luteal phase** (final week before period), emotional, physical, and behavioral symptoms.

4. Menstruation (Day 1 of next cycle):

Hormone levels drop, and **PMDD symptoms resolve** within a few days of bleeding starting.

Key distinction:

PMS and PMDD both appear in the **late luteal phase**, but PMDD is **far more severe and disruptive**, with marked mood symptoms that go away once the period starts.

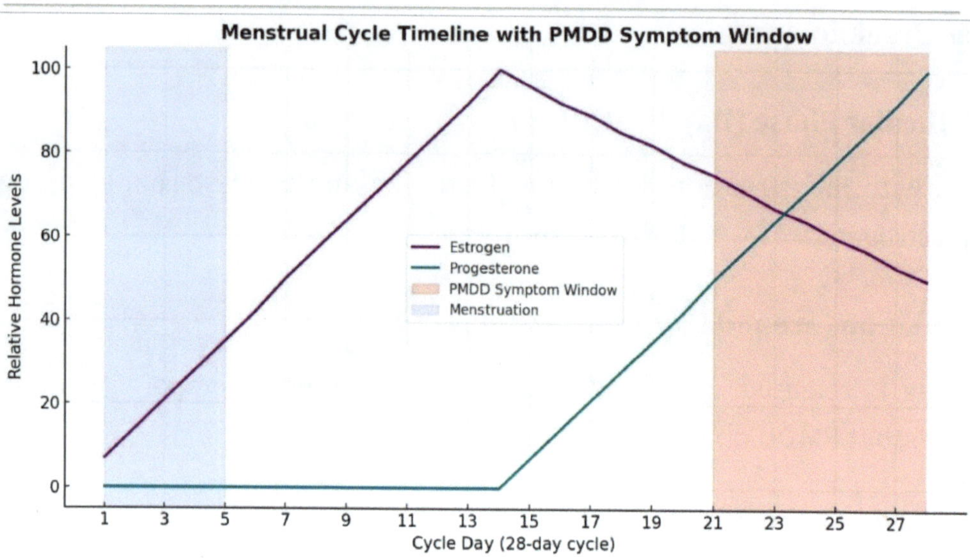
Menstrual Cycle Timeline with PMDD Symptom Window
Relative Hormone Levels
Cycle Day (28-day cycle)
Estrogen
Progesterone
PMDD Symptom Window
Menstruation

Why PMDD Is Often Misdiagnosed or Dismissed

1. General Medical Misunderstanding

- **Limited training:** Most medical and mental health providers receive very little
- education on PMDD during medical school or residency. Many confuse it with PMS or general mood disorders.
- **Overlap with psychiatric conditions:** PMDD can mimic depression, anxiety, bipolar disorder, PTSD, or borderline personality disorder. Many patients are first diagnosed with one of these instead.
- **Cycle link overlooked:** Providers often fail to connect symptoms to the menstrual cycle and therefore miss the cyclical pattern that defines PMDD.

2. Gender Bias in Medicine

- **"Hormones" dismissal:** Women and AFAB (assigned female at birth) patients are often told symptoms are "just hormones" or "normal PMS," minimizing their suffering.
- **Pain and mood bias:** Studies show women's reports of pain and mood symptoms are taken less seriously than men's, leading to delayed or inadequate treatment.

3. Stigma Around Mental Health

- **Emotional symptoms labeled as weakness:** Patients are often told to "manage stress" or "be less emotional."
- **Fear of being labeled "unstable":** Many avoid reporting the severity of mood symptoms because of stigma, especially suicidal thoughts.

Barriers in BIPOC Communities

1. Structural Racism in Healthcare

- **Less likely to be believed:** Black women in particular are historically dismissed when reporting pain, mood symptoms, or reproductive health concerns.

- **Implicit bias:** Providers may stereotype BIPOC as "angry," "dramatic," or "strong enough to handle it," reducing the chances of proper evaluation.

2. Misdiagnosis Patterns

- **BIPOC patients are more often diagnosed with Bipolar Disorder or Schizophrenia** instead of PMDD, especially when presenting with mood swings, irritability, or anger.

- **Lack of culturally informed care:** Providers may not understand how PMDD symptoms manifest differently under cultural, social, and economic stressors.

3. Access to Care

- **Insurance disparities:** Many BIPOC patients are underinsured or on public health plans with limited reproductive mental health coverage.

- **Fewer specialists:** Gynecologists or psychiatrists trained in PMDD are less accessible in communities of color.

- **Research gap:** Most PMDD studies are conducted on white populations, limiting culturally relevant diagnostic tools.

4. Cultural and Community Stigma

- **Silence around reproductive health:** In many BIPOC cultures, menstrual health is a taboo subject, making it harder to seek help.

- **Mental health stigma:** Fear of judgment or being seen as "crazy" may prevent seeking psychiatric support.

Summary

PMDD is misdiagnosed or dismissed because:

1. Providers confuse it with PMS or mood disorders.
2. Women's reproductive mental health complaints are historically minimized.
3. In BIPOC communities, **bias, stigma, and access issues** make diagnosis even harder.
4. The result is **delayed recognition**, years of untreated suffering, and inappropriate medications.

Holding Communities Accountable

PMDD, reproductive mental health, and broader equity issues don't get better without community accountability. Below are some structured ways to **hold communities, systems, and institutions accountable:**

Ways to Hold Communities Accountable

1. Awareness & Education

- **Normalize conversation:** Host workshops, panels, or community talks on PMDD and mental health.
- **Storytelling:** Encourage lived-experience voices (especially BIPOC and justiceimpacted people) to share openly.
- **Fact sheets & infographics:** Distribute easy-to-read educational materials (like the ones we created).

2. Community-Based Organizing

- **Peer advocacy groups:** Form PMDD support circles within community centers, faithbased groups, or nonprofits.
- **Coalitions:** Build alliances across reproductive justice, mental health, and racial equity organizations.
- **Community watchdogs:** Create grassroots accountability boards to monitor healthcare providers, insurers, and local agencies.

3. Accountability in Healthcare

- **Cultural competency training:** Demand providers complete training on PMDD and BIPOC health disparities.
- **Community scorecards:** Patients rate local clinics/hospitals on

responsiveness to reproductive mental health needs.

- **Data transparency:** Push for race-disaggregated data on PMDD diagnosis and treatment access.

4. Policy & Systems Change

- **Legislative advocacy:** Call for inclusion of PMDD in women's health and mental health funding streams.
- **Insurance accountability:** Hold Medi-Cal, Medicaid, and private insurers
- accountable for covering PMDD-related treatments (SSRIs, hormonal therapies, therapy, MTM meals).
- **Civil rights framing:** Treat dismissal of reproductive mental health (esp. in BIPOC women) as a health equity and civil rights issue.

5. Legal & Media Pressure

- **Complaints and grievances:** File with Civil Rights offices (like OCR, CRD, HUD) when discrimination occurs.
- **Legal support:** Partner with disability and women's rights attorneys for stronger cases.
- **Media amplification:** Use press releases, op-eds, and interviews to call out neglect and demand reform.

6. Internal Community Responsibility

- **Challenging stigma:** Confront cultural silence around menstruation and mental health within families and local organizations.
- **Mutual aid:** Build systems where women with PMDD get direct support (childcare swaps, food delivery, healing spaces).

- **Shared accountability:** Encourage men, leaders, and allies to participate in advocacy, not just those directly affected.

Bottom line:

Holding communities accountable means **education, organizing, and pressure — from inside (cultural shifts) and outside (policy, legal, media).**

PMDD doesn't just affect the person experiencing it — it impacts partners, family, and close relationships. Here's a full breakdown:

Relationship Difficulties Living with PMDD

1. Emotional Instability

- **Severe mood swings** in the late luteal phase can cause irritability, sadness, or anger outbursts that may feel unpredictable to partners.
- Partners often report feeling like they are "walking on eggshells."

2. Misunderstanding & Dismissal

- If a partner believes PMDD is "just PMS," the person with PMDD may feel **invalidated or gaslit.**
- This lack of recognition can cause resentment, distance, and deep emotional harm.

3. Communication Strain

- PMDD affects memory, focus, and regulation → leading to **arguments, miscommunication, or perceived withdrawal.**
- Partners may misinterpret withdrawal as rejection or lack of love.

4. Intimacy Challenges

- PMDD often causes fatigue, bloating, breast tenderness, or low libido.
- This can create frustration if partners don't understand that intimacy challenges are cyclical and not personal.

5. Guilt & Shame

- The person with PMDD may feel guilty for outbursts or mood swings, while partners may feel helpless, hurt, or blamed.
- This cycle of guilt can erode relationship trust if not addressed openly.

Coping with a Family Member Who Has PMDD

1. Understanding the Impact on Families

- **Mood shifts & tension:** Irritability, sadness, or anger during the luteal phase may lead to conflict at home.
- **Withdrawal & isolation:** A family member may retreat, avoid family activities, or appear distant, which can feel confusing or hurtful.
- **Role strain:** Children or siblings might take on extra responsibilities during PMDD flare-ups, leading to stress or resentment.
- **Emotional ripple effect:** Family may feel like they are "walking on eggshells," not knowing what version of their loved one they'll get.
- **Misinterpretation:** Without education, relatives may believe the person is "moody," "lazy," or "overreacting," instead of recognizing PMDD as a medical condition.

2. How Siblings Can Cope

- **Learn the cycle:** Knowing that symptoms appear before periods and fade afterward helps separate *the person* from *the disorder.*
- **Set boundaries:** It's okay to step back during heated moments, instead of escalating conflict.
- **Offer empathy, not criticism:** "I know this isn't easy for you. I'm here if you want to talk."
- **Encourage fun & normalcy:** When symptoms ease, siblings can rebuild connection through positive activities.

3. How Parents/Children Can Cope

If you are a parent of a child/teen with PMDD:

- **Validate feelings:** Teens, especially, may feel dismissed. Affirm their pain is real.
- **Support professional care:** Advocate for medical or therapeutic evaluation.
- **Help with structure:** Encourage sleep, nutrition, and school balance, while being flexible during flare-ups.
- **Watch for safety concerns:** Monitor for suicidal thoughts or self-harm. Create a crisis plan.

If you are a child of a parent with PMDD:

- **Understand it's not your fault:** The anger, withdrawal, or sadness is about PMDD, not you.
- **Don't take on adult roles:** If possible, other supportive adults should help with caregiving to protect the child from role reversal.
- **Encourage open talk:** Age-appropriate conversations ("Mom has an illness that makes her sad/angry before her period") reduce confusion.
- **Access support:** Counseling, school social workers, or trusted relatives can give children safe outlets.

4. Coping as a Whole Family

- **Cycle charting together:** Post a family calendar marking PMDD days → helps everyone anticipate.
- **Household adjustments:** Share chores or plan easier meals during symptom days.
- **Family meetings:** Brief check-ins so everyone can voice needs without blame. **Use humor & bonding:** Laughter and joy in non-PMDD weeks help reset the emotional tone.

- **Seek therapy:** Family or group counseling can reduce resentment and improve coping.

5. What to Avoid

- **Gaslighting:** Never tell them it's "just PMS" or "all in their head." • **Blame:** Avoid framing PMDD symptoms as intentional misbehavior.
- **Isolation:** Don't cut off the family member; maintain connection while respecting space.

PMDD can deeply affect siblings, children, and families — but **education, compassion, and shared coping strategies protect** relationships. Families thrive when they:

- **Recognize PMDD as medical, not personal.**
- **Work as a team to reduce stress.**
- **Balance support with healthy boundaries.**

Coping as a Couple: Supporting a Partner with PMDD

1. Educate Yourself

- Learn about PMDD symptoms and timing — **track the cycle together.**
- Understanding it's a **biological, cyclical disorder** (not a personality trait) helps reduce blame.

2. Communicate with Compassion

- Agree on a plan: "When symptoms flare, let's pause arguments until calmer."
- Use "I feel" statements instead of blame ("I feel worried when you withdraw" vs. "You always shut me out").

3. Offer Practical Support

- Help with daily tasks during the luteal phase (meals, errands, childcare).
- Encourage rest, self-care, and attending medical/therapy appointments.

4. Respect Boundaries

- If a partner says they need quiet time or space, respect that without taking it personally.
- Recognize that reduced libido or irritability is a **symptom, not rejection.**

5. Create a Crisis Plan

- If suicidal thoughts occur, know what steps to take (safety plan, crisis lines, calming strategies).
- Agree in advance on safe words or check-ins to signal when extra support is needed.

6. Focus on the "Good Weeks"

- PMDD is **cyclical**: symptoms fade after menstruation.
- Use these weeks to bond, plan enjoyable activities, and reinforce intimacy.

7. Couples Counseling or Support Groups

- A neutral space helps both partners feel heard and teaches tools to manage conflict.
- Some couples find it empowering to join PMDD support groups together.
- PMDD can strain relationships — but it doesn't have to break them.
- The most important tools are **education, compassion, teamwork, and planning.**

- With open communication and support, couples can learn to **separate the relationship from the disorder.**

PMDD doesn't just affect the individual; it can ripple through the whole family. Here's a breakdown of how PMDD impacts family dynamics, and how loved ones can cope and support:

Let's dive into **Harm Reduction**, especially as it connects to mental health, PMDD, and community accountability.

Harm Reduction 101

Definition

Harm reduction is a **set of practical strategies and principles** aimed at minimizing the negative consequences of behaviors, conditions, or systemic barriers — **without demanding perfection or abstinence.**

- Originally rooted in public health (substance use, HIV prevention).
- Now also applied to **mental health, reproductive health, and community support.**

Core Principles of Harm Reduction

1. **Meet people where they are** — support starts without judgment or ultimatums.
2. **Prioritize safety over perfection** — small steps to reduce harm are valuable.
3. **Respect lived experience** — people are the experts of their own lives.
4. **Empower choice and autonomy** — people decide what feels safe/manageable for them.
5. **Reduce stigma and shame** — validate experiences rather than dismiss them.
6. **Build trust** — through consistent, compassionate, and honest support.

Harm Reduction in Mental Health & PMDD

- **Symptom tracking** instead of expecting complete control.
- **Safety plans** (like we created) to manage suicidal urges when they arise.

- **Coping tools** (breathing, grounding, distraction) to reduce the intensity of episodes, even if symptoms don't disappear.

- **Peer support** circles that validate lived experience instead of medical dismissal.

- **Access to flexible medication plans** (e.g., SSRIs in luteal phase only) rather than "all or nothing" approaches.

- **Creating safe environments** (removing triggers, reducing isolation, adding comfort tools like weighted blankets, soothing rituals).

Harm Reduction in Healthcare

- **Language shift:** Moving away from "non-compliant" and toward "patient-centered."

- **Advocacy:** Holding providers accountable for validating PMDD and BIPOC pain reports.

- **System navigation:** Helping patients access partial services when full treatment isn't available (e.g., free clinics, peer groups, telehealth).

Harm Reduction in Community & Policy

- **Mutual aid:** Community members providing direct help (rides, meals, check-ins).

- **Policy reform:** Expanding insurance coverage and culturally competent care.

- **Decriminalization approaches:** Ensuring people with mental health crises aren't punished but supported.

- **Education campaigns:** Reducing stigma so people seek help earlier.

Harm reduction acknowledges:

- **Suffering is real.**
- **Perfection isn't the goal.**
- **Every step that makes life safer, healthier, and more manageable is progress.**

A **PMDD-specific safety plan** is a proactive, written guide that helps you recognize early warning signs and take structured steps to stay safe during your worst symptom days (late luteal phase). It is tailored to the cyclical and often severe mood shifts of PMDD.

Here's a structured draft:

PMDD Safety Plan

(Adapted for late luteal phase symptom management and suicide prevention)

1. Warning Signs (My Early Indicators)

These are thoughts, feelings, or behaviors that tell me I'm entering the danger zone:

- Sudden hopelessness or intense sadness
- Irritability or anger outbursts stronger than usual
- Feeling like a burden or worthless
- Intense physical symptoms (fatigue, pain, migraines) triggering despair
- Urge to withdraw from loved ones
- Suicidal thoughts, plans, or self-harm urges

2. Internal Coping Strategies

Things I can try on my own to calm down, distract, or ride out the symptoms:

- Breathing exercises (e.g., 4-7-8 method)
- Journaling or mood tracking to remind myself it's cyclical and temporary
- Listening to calming music or guided meditation
- Taking a warm bath/shower or using a heating pad
- Gentle exercise (walking, yoga, stretching)
- Grounding techniques (naming 5 things I see, 4 I feel, 3 I hear, 2 I smell, 1 I taste)

3. Social Supports (People I Can Contact)

- **Family/Friends:** Write names + phone numbers of trusted people who understand PMDD
- **Peer support:** A fellow PMDD warrior, support group, or online PMDD community
- **Safe spaces:** Friend's house, church, community center

4. Professional Supports (Healthcare & Crisis Contacts)

- **Therapist/Psychiatrist**: [Insert Name & Contact]
- **Primary Care or Gynecologist**: [Insert Name & Contact]
- **Emergency/Crisis Services:**
  - U.S. Suicide & Crisis Lifeline: **988**
  - Crisis Text Line: Text **HELLO** to **741741**

5. Safe Environment Plan

- Remove or lock up medications, sharp objects, or alcohol during the luteal phase
- Ask a trusted person to check in daily during the week before my period
- Keep comfort items (weighted blanket, journal, self-soothing kit) within reach

6. Reasons to Stay Alive (My Personal Anchors)

- [Write down personal motivations: children, loved ones, future goals, faith, advocacy work, unfinished projects]
- Reminder: **"This is hormonal, temporary, and treatable. It will pass."**

Important Note: PMDD symptoms are **time-limited**. Intense suicidal thoughts typically resolve once menstruation starts. This plan helps keep you safe until symptoms ease.

The relationship between **PMDD and substance use disorder (SUD)** is important and often overlooked. Here's a detailed explanation:

PMDD and Substance Use Disorder: The Connection

1. Symptom Relief & Self-Medication

- PMDD causes **intense physical and emotional distress** (depression, anxiety, irritability, pain).
- Without effective treatment or recognition, many people **self-medicate** with substances such as:
    - **Alcohol** (to numb emotional pain or improve sleep)
    - **Cannabis** (to manage mood swings, anxiety, or cramps)
    - **Nicotine** (to relieve stress, though it can worsen anxiety long-term)
    - **Prescription misuse** (e.g., painkillers, sedatives during luteal phase)
- This **self-medication cycle** increases the risk of dependence and long-term SUD.

2. Shared Risk Factors

- **Mood disorders:** PMDD is strongly linked to depression and anxiety, which are themselves risk factors for substance use.
- **Trauma history:** Many people with PMDD also have histories of trauma or PTSD, which elevate risk for both PMDD severity and SUD.
- **Impulsivity & dysregulation:** PMDD's late luteal phase can cause poor impulse control, making substance use more likely.

3. Cycle-Specific Vulnerability

- **Late luteal phase:** Cravings and urges may intensify right before menstruation when symptoms peak.
- **Withdrawal overlap:** Substance withdrawal can mimic or worsen PMDD symptoms (irritability, anxiety, mood swings), creating a **vicious cycle** that complicates diagnosis.

4. Disparities & Dismissal

- **Medical gaslighting:** When PMDD symptoms are dismissed as "PMS," individuals may turn to substances instead of receiving appropriate medical care.
- **BIPOC women** face even greater barriers — systemic racism and stigma increase both misdiagnosis and vulnerability to self-medicating.

5. Treatment & Harm Reduction Approaches

- **Integrated care is crucial:** Treating PMDD and SUD separately often fails — both conditions must be addressed together.
- **SSRIs and hormonal stabilization** may reduce the emotional triggers that lead to substance use.
- **Harm reduction strategies** (safe substance use education, support groups, traumainformed care) help reduce risks while managing PMDD.
- **Peer support and accountability** (12-step groups, SMART Recovery, or PMDDspecific support circles) can provide validation and healthier coping.

PMDD doesn't directly "cause" substance use disorder, but its **intense, cyclical suffering** makes people **far more vulnerable to self-medicating**, which can lead to dependency.

The safest path is **integrated harm reduction + medical treatment** — treating both PMDD and substance use as **real, valid conditions** requiring compassion and support.

An important angle — and often missing in mainstream discussions- here is a deep dive into the connection between PMDD, substance use, and justice-impacted individuals:

PMDD & Justice-Impacted Individuals

1. Criminalization of Symptoms

- **Behavioral symptoms of PMDD** — irritability, anger outbursts, impulsivity, risky behavior — can lead to conflict at home, work, or in public.
- When misunderstood, these behaviors may result in **arrests for disorderly conduct, assault, or self-defense scenarios** where PMDD is never considered.
- Instead of treatment, many individuals with PMDD are punished, reinforcing cycles of criminalization.

2. Self-Medication & Substance-Related Charges

- **High rates of self-medication** in PMDD (alcohol, cannabis, prescription misuse) increase vulnerability to **drug-related arrests, DUIs, and probation/parole violations.**
- Harmful behaviors driven by **late luteal phase crises** (e.g., self-harm in public, intoxication to numb pain) are often criminalized instead of treated as mental health episodes.

3. Incarceration & Misdiagnosis

- Women and AFAB individuals in jails/prisons are **rarely screened for PMDD.**
- PMDD may be misdiagnosed as **bipolar disorder, borderline personality disorder, or "behavioral problems."**
- Inside correctional settings, cycles of **untreated PMDD can worsen aggression, despair, or suicide risk.**

4. Intersection with Trauma

- Justice-impacted women often have **histories of trauma, abuse, and systemic neglect.**

Trauma worsens PMDD severity, while PMDD increases vulnerability to self-destructive behaviors — creating a feedback loop that feeds incarceration.

5. Disparities in BIPOC Communities

- Black, Indigenous, and Latine women face higher rates of arrest, harsher sentencing, and medical dismissal.

- PMDD-related crises in BIPOC individuals are more likely to be seen as **criminal behavior** instead of symptoms requiring care.

6. Reentry & Recidivism

- Without recognition of PMDD, justice-impacted individuals leaving incarceration:

    - Struggle with untreated symptoms that interfere with probation or parole compliance.

    - Are vulnerable to relapse into substance use, especially during luteal phase crises.

    - Face stigma and barriers in accessing reproductive mental health care, increasing risk of re-incarceration.

7. Pathways for Harm Reduction & Justice Reform

- **Screening:** Mandate PMDD screening in correctional facilities and diversion programs.

- **Diversion:** Expand **mental health diversion** (like your case in Hollywood Mental Health Court) to include PMDD-specific accommodations.

- **Medical Care in Custody:** Ensure access to SSRIs, hormonal treatments, and peer support for PMDD inside facilities.

- **Training for Courts & Corrections:** Judges, probation officers, and staff must learn to recognize PMDD as a legitimate condition.
- **Advocacy:** Reframe PMDD not as "anger" or "attitude," but as a **recognized medical disorder** requiring treatment, not punishment.

Justice-impacted individuals with PMDD are caught at the intersection of **gender bias, medical neglect, and systemic criminalization.**

- Their symptoms are often misread as **criminal behavior** rather than a **disabling psychiatric condition.**
- Recognizing PMDD in this population is a **civil rights issue** — tied to healthcare equity, decarcerating, and trauma-informed justice reform.

Emotional Support Animals (ESAs) can play a crucial role for people living with PMDD. Here's a deep explanation:

The Need for Emotional Support Animals in PMDD

1. Why Emotional Support Is Critical

- PMDD causes **severe mood dysregulation, hopelessness, anxiety, and irritability** during the late luteal phase.
- Many report feeling **isolated, misunderstood, or dismissed** by medical professionals, family, or partners.
- This makes **consistent, non-judgmental companionship** extremely valuable.

2. How ESAs Help with PMDD

- **Grounding & Comfort:** The presence of an ESA provides immediate emotional grounding during panic, rage, or despair episodes.
- **Routine & Stability:** Caring for an animal enforces a daily structure, which helps regulate sleep, activity, and stress.
- **Non-Judgmental Support:** Unlike human interactions, animals provide unconditional acceptance, reducing feelings of rejection.
- **Physical Soothing:** Petting or cuddling animals releases **oxytocin and serotonin**, hormones that counteract PMDD-related mood crashes.
- **Distraction from Symptoms:** Interaction with an ESA shifts attention away from negative thought spirals.
- **Safety Buffer:** For those experiencing **suicidal ideation**, an ESA may serve as a protective factor — a reason to hold on, care, and survive the worst days.

3. Legal Recognition of ESAs

- Under the **Fair Housing Act (FHA)**, individuals with disabling conditions (including psychiatric conditions like PMDD) may qualify for ESA accommodations (waived pet fees, housing approval).

- PMDD is recognized in the DSM-5 as a **depressive disorder**, which supports documentation for ESA letters.

- An ESA does not require specialized training (unlike a service animal), but it does require a **letter from a licensed mental health professional.**

4. Why PMDD Warrants ESA Access

- **Cycle-based disability:** PMDD causes **predictable, disabling symptoms** every month, severely impairing relationships, work, and self-care.

- **High suicide risk:** Research shows women with PMDD have a **significantly elevated risk of suicidal thoughts and attempts.** An ESA can help reduce risk.

- **Limited treatments:** Since medications don't work for everyone (and some carry side effects), ESAs offer a **holistic, supportive intervention.**

5. Recommendations

- **Healthcare providers:** Should consider ESA letters as part of a comprehensive PMDD treatment plan.

- **Courts, schools, and housing authorities:** Need to recognize ESA accommodations for those with PMDD as a matter of disability rights.

- **Individuals with PMDD:** Can track symptom relief with their ESA to strengthen medical documentation.

For individuals living with PMDD, an Emotional Support Animal can mean the difference between **isolation and connection, despair and survival.**

ESAs provide **unconditional grounding, routine, and emotional stability** during cyclical mental health crises — making them an essential, not optional, part of care.

PMDD in the Workplace

PMDD in the workplace is a major issue, and one of the most invisible forms of discrimination people face. Here's a deep breakdown:

1. Why It's a Workplace Issue

- PMDD is not just "PMS" — it is a **cyclical, disabling psychiatric condition** recognized in the DSM-5.
- It causes **severe mood symptoms (irritability, anxiety, depression, brain fog)** plus **physical symptoms (pain, fatigue, migraines)**.
- These symptoms strike **7–14 days each month**, affecting job performance, attendance, and interpersonal relationships.

2. Common Workplace Challenges

- **Absenteeism:** Missing work due to extreme fatigue, migraines, or suicidal thoughts.
- **Presenteeism:** Being physically present but unable to focus/productive due to brain fog or pain.
- **Conflict with coworkers/supervisors:** Irritability, anger outbursts, or withdrawal may be misinterpreted as attitude problems.
- **Performance reviews:** PMDD symptoms can cause cyclical dips in output, often misunderstood as inconsistency or lack of professionalism.
- **Fear of disclosure:** Many don't tell employers about PMDD due to stigma, sexism, or fear of retaliation.
- **Discrimination:** BIPOC employees may be dismissed at higher rates ("angry," "lazy," or "unreliable"), leading to job loss or blocked advancement.

3. Legal Protections

- **PMDD as a disability:** Under the **ADA (Americans with Disabilities Act)**, PMDD can qualify as a disability if it substantially limits major life activities (work, social functioning, focus, self-care).
- **FMLA (Family and Medical Leave Act):** Employees may qualify for protected leave during severe episodes.
- **Reasonable accommodations:** Employers are required to provide accommodations if PMDD is disclosed and documented.

4. Possible Workplace Accommodations

- **Flexible scheduling:** Adjusting work hours during the luteal phase or allowing remote work.
- **Modified workload:** Temporary reduction or reassignment of tasks during severe symptom days.
- **Rest breaks & wellness spaces:** Access to quiet rooms, heat packs, hydration, or time for grounding practices.
- **Leave options:** Intermittent leave under FMLA or sick leave banks.
- **Supportive culture:** Supervisor and HR training to recognize PMDD as medical, not behavioral.

5. Coping Strategies for Employees

- **Cycle tracking:** Helps anticipate symptom days and plan workloads.
- **Proactive communication:** If safe, share needs with HR or a trusted supervisor.
- **Self-care planning:** Use wellness tools (hydration, healthy snacks, breaks, grounding techniques) at work.

- **Peer support:** Connect with coworkers or employee resource groups for advocacy and solidarity.

6. Coping Strategies for Employers/Managers

- **Educate & train:** Learn about PMDD to reduce stigma.
- **Accommodate, don't punish:** Recognize that cyclical performance dips are medical, not motivational.
- **Normalize flexibility:** Hybrid work, wellness policies, and menstrual health equity initiatives support all employees.
- **Promote equity:** Ensure BIPOC and marginalized employees are not disproportionately disciplined for PMDD-related issues.

PMDD is a **workplace equity issue**. Without recognition, employees are punished for symptoms of a disabling condition. With **education, accommodations, and compassion**, workplaces can reduce stigma, improve productivity, and protect the rights of those living with PMDD.

PMDD IN THE WORKPLACE

Currently, **no public data ranks insurance companies by how much care they specifically provide for women with PMDD**. However, some insurers and providers stand out for offering more accessible, structured, and responsive PMDD-related coverage. Here's what the evidence shows:

Insurers & Providers with Strong PMDD Coverage

Aetna

- Aetna's clinical policy bulletins explicitly recognize PMDD as a medically necessary condition, covering both diagnostic and treatment services, including psychiatric evaluation, SSRIs, hormonal therapies, and even surgical options in extreme cases. (Aetna)

Telehealth Providers Accepting Major Insurers

- **Brightside Health** offers tailored PMDD treatment through psychiatry and therapy, and accepts many major insurers—Aetna, Cigna, United Healthcare, Anthem, BCBS. (Brightside)

- **Reimagine Psychiatry** in California accepts Aetna, Anthem Blue Cross/Blue Shield, and other major carriers for telehealth PMDD treatment. (Reimagine Psychiatry)

CVS MinuteClinic (Aetna Plan Holders)

- MinuteClinic locations—within CVS—offer menstrual health support, including PMS/PMDD evaluations and treatments. Most Aetna plans cover these services, with no extra cost for birth control.

  (Aetna)

Life Stance Health

- Provides in-person and telehealth care for PMDD. Federal mental health parity laws require insurers to cover counseling and medication for mental health conditions just like physical health. LifeStance accepts most insurance plans. (LifeStance Health)

Key Insights

Insurer / Provider	PMDD Recognition & Coverage	Accepts Multiple Insurers
Aetna	Yes — covers diagnostics & treatments clinical policy (Aetna)	— per
Brightside Health	Yes — tailored psychiatry + therapy	Receives Aetna, Cigna, UHC, Anthem, BCBS (Brightside)
Reimagine Psychiatry	Yes — PMDD treatment via telehealth	Accepts Aetna, Anthem, BCBS (Reimagine Psychiatry)
MinuteClinic (CVS)	Offers PMDD support under Aetna plans	Available to Aetna subscribers (Aetna)
Life Stance Health	Yes — offers therapy and medication	Accepts most insurance per parity law (Life Stance Health)

Summary

- **Aetna** stands out with explicit PMDD policy support, covering a wide range of treatments.
- **Brightside**, **Reimagine**, **MinuteClinic**, and **Life Stance** provide accessible, insurersupported services that facilitate PMDD care.
- **Telehealth options** are particularly valuable for improving access,

especially for individuals in underserved areas or communities.

Here's what Medi-Cal covers—and how it relates to PMDD care:

Medi-Cal Mental Health Coverage: Overview

Broad Scope of Mental Health Services

Medi-Cal covers a wide range of behavioral and mental health services, including:

- Individual and group psychotherapy
- Psychiatric evaluations and assessments
- Medication management
- Crisis intervention
- Specialty Mental Health Services (SMHS) provided through county Mental Health Plans (MHPs) for individuals meeting medical necessity criteria

  (DMHC, California Health Care Foundation, Grow Therapy)

These services are part of Medi-Cal's commitment to mental health parity, ensuring behavioral health benefits are comparable to medical benefits.

(DMHC)

Delivery System

- **Managed Care Plans (MCPs)** offer non-specialty outpatient mental health services for mild-to-moderate conditions.
- More intensive **Specialty Mental Health Services (SMHS)** are provided by county MHPs to those who qualify based on medical necessity.

(California Pan-Ethnic Health Network, California Health Care Foundation)

Members can access moderate care directly—without PCP referrals—and urgent mental health appointments must be provided within 2 business days; non-urgent within 10 days. (California Pan-Ethnic Health Network)

PMDD: Where It Fits in Medi-Cal

Is PMDD Covered?

- **Yes**—PMDD is a **recognized mental health condition (DSM-5)** requiring treatment like therapy, medication, and psychiatric evaluation.
- Medi-Cal's mental health services include these interventions, meaning PMDD-related outpatient care is **covered under both MCP and SMHS pathways**, depending on severity and medical necessity.

  (MGH Women's Mental Health Center, California Health Care Foundation)

Access Considerations

- **Mild-to-Moderate Impact:** PMDD symptoms that disrupt daily life but don't meet severe impairment criteria are typically covered via MCPs.
- **Severe Cases:** If symptoms significantly impair functioning, individuals may be eligible for SMHS with county MHPs. (California Health Care Foundation)

Barriers to Access

- Many PCPs and Medi-Cal members are unaware of the expanded mental health benefits, making referrals and access challenging.
- Documentation, provider availability, and disparities—especially among BIPOC, nonEnglish speakers, and rural communities—create **access**

gaps.

(California Pan-Ethnic Health Network)

Summary Table

Aspect	**Details**
Treatment Coverage	Outpatient therapy, meds, psychiatric evaluation—covered under MediCal
Service Pathways	Managed Care (MCP) for mild-to-moderate; County MHPs (SMHS) for severe PMDD
Access Rights	No referral needed; timely appointment guarantees in place
Common Barriers	Awareness, provider shortages, systemic disparities in access

Medi-Cal does cover PMDD treatment; individuals should qualify for **therapy, medication, and psychiatric care** as medically necessary mental health services. Whether under Managed Care or Specialty Mental Health, PMDD-related treatment is eligible for coverage.

Meals & Beverages

"Every step you take to nourish your body is also a step toward healing your mind and spirit. Let food be your medicine, and let each meal remind you of your strength."

Here's a 7-day PMDD-focused meal plan designed to help regulate hormone imbalance, support serotonin production, reduce inflammation, and stabilize blood sugar (all critical for PMDD symptom management). I've structured it with whole foods, steady protein, healthy fats, and hormone-friendly micronutrients.

PMDD Hormone-Balancing Meal Plan

Guiding Principles:

- Protein at every meal → stabilizes blood sugar and reduces mood swings.
- Complex carbs + fiber → boost serotonin and balance estrogen
- Omega-3s & healthy fats → reduce inflammation, support brain health.
- Magnesium-rich foods (pumpkin seeds, spinach, quinoa) → calm mood, ease cramps.
- Calcium + vitamin D → supports bone and hormone health.
- Avoid: excess caffeine, alcohol, processed sugar, refined carbs, and high-salt foods (they worsen bloating, anxiety, and mood).

Day 1 Breakfast: Oatmeal with chia seeds, walnuts, and blueberries (magnesium + omega3s). Lunch: Quinoa salad with chickpeas, spinach, cucumbers, and olive oil-lemon dressing. Snack: Pumpkin seeds + sliced apple. Dinner: Grilled salmon, roasted sweet potato, and steamed broccoli. Evening: Chamomile tea.

Day 2 Breakfast: Greek yogurt with flaxseeds, raspberries, and a drizzle of honey. Lunch: Lentil soup with a side of mixed greens. Snack: Hummus with carrot and celery sticks. Dinner: Baked chicken breast, brown rice, and sautéed kale with garlic. Evening: Warm golden milk (turmeric + almond milk)

Day 3 Breakfast: Scrambled eggs with spinach and avocado on whole-grain toast. Lunch: Wild rice bowl with black beans, roasted zucchini, and tahini drizzle. Snack: Handful of almonds + pear. Dinner: Grilled trout, roasted beets, and quinoa. Evening: Peppermint tea (helps with bloating).

Day 4 Breakfast: Smoothie with banana, spinach, protein powder, almond butter, and ground flaxseed. Lunch: Turkey & avocado wrap with whole-grain tortilla, lettuce, and tomato. Snack: Greek yogurt + pumpkin seeds. Dinner: Baked cod, roasted Brussels sprouts, and mashed cauliflower. Evening: Rooibos tea.

Day 5 Breakfast: Steel-cut oats with sunflower seeds, strawberries, and cinnamon. Lunch: Chickpea curry with brown rice. Snack: Rice cakes with almond butter. Dinner: Grilled shrimp, quinoa tabbouleh, and sautéed green beans. Evening: Warm ginger tea.

Day 6 Breakfast: Cottage cheese with sliced peaches and chia seeds. Lunch: Mixed greens with grilled chicken, walnuts, cranberries, and balsamic vinaigrette. Snack: Dark chocolate square (70%+) + handful of cashews. Dinner: Baked turkey meatballs with zucchini noodles and marinara (no added sugar). Evening: Lavender tea.

Day 7 Breakfast: Avocado toast with poached egg and arugula. Lunch: Buddha bowl (quinoa, roasted sweet potato, kale, pumpkin seeds, tahini). Snack: Sliced cucumber + hummus. Dinner:

Grilled salmon with wild rice and steamed asparagus. Evening: Warm almond milk with cinnamon.

PMDD Meals (5)

1. Salmon with Roasted Brussels Sprouts
2. Quinoa Bowl with Spinach & Roasted Sweet Potatoes
3. Chicken with Turmeric Brown Rice & Broccoli
4. Greek Yogurt with Berries & Walnuts
5. Lentil Soup with Kale & Carrots

Vegan Versions (5)

1. Chickpea Steaks with Roasted Brussels Sprouts
2. Quinoa Bowl with Spinach & Roasted Sweet Potatoes (vegan dressing)

3. Turmeric Brown Rice with Tempeh & Broccoli
4. Coconut Yogurt with Berries & Walnuts
5. Lentil & Kale Soup with Carrots

Smoothies & On-the-Go Meal Replacements (5)

1. Anti-Inflammatory Turmeric Mango Smoothie
2. Hormone-Balancing Berry Maca Smoothie
3. Omega-Boost Green Avocado Smoothie
4. Chocolate Protein Almond Shake
5. Fiber-Rich Chia & Oatmeal Smoothie

Supplements & Support (general guidance)

- Magnesium glycinate or citrate (calms mood, reduces cramps/bloating)
- Vitamin B6 (supports serotonin and progesterone balance)
- Calcium + Vitamin D (especially if dairy-free)
- Omega-3 fish oil (supports mood & hormone balance)
- Adaptogens (ashwagandha, rhodiola, chasteberry) – with provider approval.

PMDD 7-Day Meal Plan Grocery List

Proteins • Salmon fillets • Chicken breast • Turkey breast / ground turkey • Shrimp • Cod or Trout • Eggs

Grains & Legumes • Quinoa • Brown rice • Wild rice • Lentils • Chickpeas • Whole-grain bread or tortillas

Fruits • Blueberries • Raspberries • Strawberries • Bananas • Apples • Pears • Peaches • Cranberries (unsweetened, dried or fresh)

Vegetables • Spinach • Kale • Broccoli • Brussels sprouts • Cauliflower • Zucchini • Sweet potatoes • Asparagus • Mixed greens (spring mix, romaine, etc.) • Cucumbers • Carrots • Celery • Beets • Green beans s • Arugula • Tomatoes

Nuts & Seeds • Walnuts • Almonds • Cashews • Pumpkin seeds • Sunflower seeds • Chia seeds • Flaxseeds

Dairy & Alternatives • Greek yogurt (unsweetened) • Cottage cheese • Almond milk (unsweetened)

Pantry & Seasonings • Olive oil • Tahini • Honey • Cinnamon • Turmeric • Garlic • Ginger

Herbal Teas • Chamomile tea • Peppermint tea • Rooibos tea • Lavender tea

Recipes & Nutrition for Hormone Balance

This chapter provides practical, holistic recipes designed to support hormone balance, reduce inflammation, and stabilize energy levels for individuals managing PMDD and related conditions. These recipes emphasize whole foods, anti-inflammatory ingredients, and nutrient-dense choices. They are not medical prescriptions but tools to nourish the body and mind.

Guidelines for Hormone-Supportive Eating

- Balance blood sugar: Pair protein, healthy fats, and fiber with every meal.
- Reduce inflammation: Use anti-inflammatory foods like turmeric, ginger, leafy greens, and omega-3s.
- Support liver detox: Include cruciferous vegetables, beets, garlic, and onions.
- Mind gut health: Eat fermented foods (yogurt, kefir, sauerkraut) and fiber-rich prebiotics.
- Hydration & herbal support: Drink plenty of water, teas like chamomile or ginger. Super Woman Smoothie

Ingredients:

- 1 cup water + 1/2 cup milk of choice
- 2 Brazil nuts
- 4 pitted dates
- 1/2 frozen banana
- 1/2 cup blueberries
- 1/2 cup spinach or kale

- 1 Tbsp tahini
- 1 Tbsp hemp seeds
- 1 Tbsp cacao nibs or 1/2 Tbsp cacao powder
- 1 tsp maca powder
- 1 tsp coconut oil or avocado

Instructions: Blend all ingredients until creamy. A nutrient powerhouse with protein, healthy fats, and adaptogens.

Hormone-Balancing Morning Smoothie Ingredients:

- 1 cup almond milk (unsweetened)
- 1/2 cup plain Greek yogurt (or non- dairy)
- 1/2 cup frozen berries
- 1/2 ripe banana
- 1 Tbsp flaxseed
- 1 Tbsp chia seeds
- 1 Tbsp almond butter
- 1 tsp maca powder
- 1/2 tsp cinnamon
- 1/4 tsp turmeric

Instructions: Blend until smooth. Rich in anti-inflammatory spices and hormone-friendly seeds.

Berry & Greens Smoothie Bowl Ingredients:

- 1 cup frozen mixed berries
- 1/2 banana
- 1 cup spinach
- 1/2 avocado
- 1 Tbsp chia seeds
- 1 Tbsp almond butter
- 1/2 cup nut milk

Instructions: Blend into thick consistency. Top with granola, coconut flakes, or fresh fruit. Golden Turmeric Latte

Ingredients:

- 1 cup coconut or almond milk
- 1/2 tsp turmeric
- 1/4 tsp ginger powder
- 1/4 tsp cinnamon
- 1 tsp honey or maple syrup

Instructions: Warm milk gently, whisk in spices and sweetener. Anti-inflammatory comfort drink. Overnight Chia Pudding Ingredients:

- 1/4 cup chia seeds
- 1 cup almond milk
- 1/2 tsp vanilla
- 1 tsp maple syrup

- Toppings: berries, nuts, coconut

Instructions: Mix seeds, milk, vanilla, and syrup. Refrigerate overnight, top with fruit before serving. Salmon with Roasted Brussels Sprouts Ingredients:

- 1 salmon filet
- 1 cup Brussels sprouts, halved
- 1 Tbsp olive oil
- 1/2 tsp turmeric
- Salt & pepper

Instructions: Roast sprouts at 400°F for 20 min. Pan-sear salmon with olive oil, season with turmeric, salt, and pepper. Lentil Vegetable Stew Ingredients:

- 1 cup lentils
- 2 carrots, chopped
- 2 celery stalks, chopped
- 1 onion, diced
- 1 tsp garlic
- 1 tsp turmeric
- 1 tsp cumin
- 6 cups vegetable broth

Instructions: Sauté onion, garlic, and spices. Add veggies, broth, lentils. Simmer 30 minutes. Avocado & Hummus Wrap

Ingredients:

- 1 whole grain or collard wrap
- 1/4 avocado, sliced
- 2 Tbsp hummus
- 1/2 cup mixed greens
- 1/4 cup shredded carrots

Instructions: Spread hummus on wrap, add veggies and avocado, roll tightly. Quinoa & Veggie Bowl Ingredients:

- 1 cup cooked quinoa
- 1/2 cup roasted broccoli
- 1/2 cup roasted sweet potato
- 1 Tbsp pumpkin seeds
- Tahini drizzle

Instructions: Layer ingredients in bowl, drizzle with tahini. Rich in fiber and minerals. Bone Broth Vegetable Soup

Ingredients:

- 4 cups bone broth (chicken or beef)
- 1 zucchini, chopped
- 1 carrot, chopped
- 1/2 onion, diced
- 2 garlic cloves

Instructions: Simmer broth with veggies and garlic 30 min. Nourishing and gut-supportive. Hormone-Friendly Oats Ingredients:

- 1/2 cup rolled oats
- 1 cup almond milk
- 1 Tbsp flaxseed meal
- 1 Tbsp almond butter
- 1/2 tsp cinnamon
- 1/2 cup berries

Instructions: Cook oats in milk, stir in flaxseed and almond butter, top with berries. Stuffed Sweet Potato Ingredients:

- 1 baked sweet potato
- 1/2 cup black beans
- 1/4 avocado
- 1 Tbsp salsa
- Cilantro garnish

Instructions: Split potato, stuff with beans, avocado, and salsa. Nutrient-rich comfort food. Herbal Hormone Balance Tea Blend Ingredients:

- 1 tsp dried chamomile
- 1 tsp dried ginger
- 1 tsp peppermint leaves
- Hot water

Instructions: Steep herbs in hot water 10 minutes. Calming and hormone-supportive. Instructions: Layer ingredients in bowl, drizzle with tahini. Rich in fiber and minerals. Bone Broth Vegetable Soup Ingredients:

- 4 cups bone broth (chicken or beef)
- 1 zucchini, chopped
- 1 carrot, chopped
- 1/2 onion, diced
- 2 garlic cloves

Instructions: Simmer broth with veggies and garlic 30 min. Nourishing and gut-supportive. Hormone-Friendly Oats Ingredients:

- 1/2 cup rolled oats
- 1 cup almond milk
- 1 Tbsp flaxseed meal
- 1 Tbsp almond butter
- 1/2 tsp cinnamon
- 1/2 cup berries

Instructions: Cook oats in milk, stir in flaxseed and almond butter, top with berries. Stuffed Sweet Potato Ingredients:

- 1 baked sweet potato
- 1/2 cup black beans
- 1/4 avocado
- 1 Tbsp salsa

- Cilantro garnish

Instructions: Split potato, stuff with beans, avocado, and salsa. Nutrient-rich comfort food. Herbal Hormone Balance Tea Blend Ingredients:

- 1 tsp dried chamomile
- 1 tsp dried ginger
- 1 tsp peppermint leaves
- Hot water

Instructions: Steep herbs in hot water 10 minutes. Calming and hormone-supportive. Mediterranean Power Bowl Ingredients:

- 1/2 cup cooked farro
- 1/2 cup chickpeas
- 1/2 cup cucumber and tomato salad
- 2 Tbsp hummus
- 1 Tbsp olive oil drizzle

Instructions: Assemble bowl with all components, drizzle with olive oil.

Anti-Inflammatory Golden Latte

Sencee: 1
Prop Time: 1 minutes
Cook Time: 3 minutes

Ingredieate

- 1-cap-unsweetened eat milk (or milk of choice)
- 1-2-cap ground snmeric
- 1+2-ap-ground cinnamon
- Simal plach of black arwner
- 1+2-eip honey or mople sorup (optionel)

Stope

1. Combine sot milk, turmeric, ginger, cinnarto, cinnamon, black prmper, honey of harge, *lme vear tllsecoes auo*
2. Which couvmedium *Nath* with steaming and warmed through. *(ber 4uobrp 8Bo,*
3. Peur oncro rvap and or adjust sweetiness to taste.
4. From with a milk mother or imimettion blender in blender.

Outcome: Wann: spiced, creamy turmeric drink with anti-(ithamonsor) and ruitrunsato propenie:

Nutrition Nates: Turmeric and grger anc-reduce (iflamimation, black papper enhances afssonation of corcomm efaces.

PMDD-RELIEF

FRUITS AND VEGETABLES FOR DRINKS & SMOOTHIES

PMDD-RELIEF

NUTRITIONAL SUPPORT FOR PREMENSTRUAL DYSPHORIC DISORDER

SUPPORTIVE FOODS

- Fiber-rich vegetables (broccoli, carrots, kale)
- Leafy greens (spinach, chard, collard greens)
- Lentils and legumes
- Low-glycemic fruits (berries-apples)
- Omega-3-rich foods (salmon, walnuts, flaxseed)
- Probiotic foods (yogurt, sauerkraut)

SUPPLEMENTS

- Magnesium (400–600 mg/day)
- Calcium (500–1000 mg/day)
- Vitamin B6 (50–100 mg/day)
- Omega-3 fatty acids
- Vitamin D

LIMIT

- Sugar and refined carbohydrates
- Caffeine
- Alcohol

LIMIT

- Sugar and refined carbohydrates
- Caffeine
- Alcohol

DETOX + GLOW ELIXIR

DETOXIFYING JUICE FOR SKIN, HORMO-
ENERGY, AND DIGESTION

SHOPPING LIST

Vegetables

- 2 medium beets (peeled and chopped)
- 3-4 large carrots (washed, trimmed)
- 3 celery stalks
- 1 cucumber (peeled, if waxed)

Fruits

- 1 cup pineapple chunks (fresh or frozen)
- 2 oranges (peeled)
- 1 green or ed apple (cored)
- ½ cup red grapes
- 1 lemon (peeled)
- 1 lime (peeled)

Roots + Boosters

- 1-inch piece ginger (peeled)
- 1-inch piece turmeric root (or ½ tsp ground turmeric)
- 1-2 tsp raw honey (optional)

INSTRUCTIONS

1. Wash and prep ail ingredients,
2. Juice in a high-quality juicer OR blend with 1-2 cups water and strain through nut milk bag or fine sieve.
3. Stir in raw honey after juicing,
4. Pour into glass jars. Store up to 48 hrs in the fridge (best fresh)

OPTIONAL ADD-INS (BONUS BENEFITS)

- Chia seeds (fiber + omega-3s)
- Black pepper (helps absorb turmeric's curcumin
- Mint or basil leaves (cooling & digestive

ULTIMATE HEALING JUICE & SMOOTHIE BLEND

Supports: Energy · Skin Clarity · Hormone Balance · Gut & Heart Health · Detox · Immuncy

Ingredients (per serving or batch):

- ✓ 1 small Beet, peeled & chopped
- ✓ 2 Carrots, peeled
- ✓ 1-2 stalks Celery
- ✓ 1 tsp Fresh Ginge grated
- ✓ 1/2 tsp Fresh Termeric or ¼ tsp powder
- ✓ Juice of 1 Lemon
- ✓ Juice of 1 Lime
- ✓ ½ cup Pineapplle Juice
- ✓ ½ cup Orange Juice
- ✓ ¼ cup Apple Juice
- ✓ ½ cup Protein Powder (plant-based or whey)
- ✓ 1 Banana
- ✓ 1 scoop Protein Powder (plant-based or whey)
- ✓ ½ cup Greek or Plant-Based Yogurt
- ✓ ½ cup Coconut Water or Milk
- ✓ 1-2 tbsp Fresh Opcnonat Meat (opptional)

Key Benfits by Category:

Ingredient	Benefit
Beets, Carrots	Liver detox, blood buitding, skin glow
Gelery, Cucumber	Anti-inflammatory, hydrating, reduces bloating
Ginger, Turmeric	Gut health, pain relief, immune boost
Citrus (lemon.	Detox, vitamin C. alkalizing
Pineapple, Apple, Grape Juice	Antioxidants, enzymes, skin & heart support
	Energy, potassium, mood, fiber
Banana	Muscle repair, hormone balance, fullness
Protein Powder	Gut support, probiotics, creamy texture

HOLDING COMMUNITIES ACCOUNTABLE

AWARENESS & EDUCATION

- Normalize conversation, hosting workhops, panels, or community talks on PMDD
- Encourage storytelling: lived-experience voices
- Distribute fact sheets/Infogs

COMMUNITY-BASED ORGANIZING

- Form PMDD support circles within community centers, falth-based groups, or nonprofits
- Grassrools accountas fintly þeard 10 motior rmental healthcare providers, insurers, or

ACCOUNTABILITY IN HEALTHCARE

- Demand providers complete **cultural competency** training on PMDD and BIPOC health disparities
- **Community scorecards:** Patients rate local clinics/nospitals on responsiveriess to reprio-ductive mental health needs
- Push for race-disaggregated data D PMDD diagnosis and treatment access

POLICY & SYSTEMS CHANGE

- **Legislative advocacy:** File proopie's PMDD nalogs with OCR, CRD. HUD when discrimination
- **Insurance accountability:** Hold Medi-Cal, Medicald, & private insurers accountable for covering **PMDD**-related treatments (SSRIs, hormonal therapies, therapy, MTM mals)
- **Civil rights:** Treating dismissal of reproductive mental health tespecially in BIPOC women) as a health equity and civil rights issue

INTERNAL COMMUNITY RESPONSIBILITY

- **Challenging stigma:** Confronting fultural silence around menstruation and rnental health within familes and local organizations
- **Mutual aid:** Building yslems where women with PMDD

PMS vs PMDD

(Premenstrual Dysphoric Disorder)

Diagnosis

PLBD	**Criteria** Symptoms recuiter during luteal phase (1-2 weeks before period) but not severe DSM-5 diagnesis)-last 5 symptoms, ncluding 1 morer mood-related symptoms (depression, anxisty, irritability, or moud swings)
Symptom Tracking	**Symptom Tracking** Often based on self-report Requires daily ratings for 22 cycles (to confirm symptoms are cyclic and severe
Impact on Life	**Impact on Life** Mild to moderate, symptoms do not severely impair daily life
Assoisted Risks	**Associated Risks** Usually no long-term mental health risk

Treatment Approaches

	Lifestyle & Self-Care Exercise, stress reduction, good sleep Limiting caffine/kak/alcohol
OTC	**Dietary Supplements** Calcium, magnesium, vitamin B5, cmega-5 fairy acids Sometives help as supportive but not enough
Hormonal Options	**Hormonal Options** Some birth control pills regulate cycle Lessen PMS Higher risk of suicict ome (not mot mud sym)
Therapy	**Psychiatric Medication** Usually not needed SBRIs (antidepress(sants) First-line treatment Taken daily or only durial luteal phase
Advanced Options	**Advanced Options** Rarely required In severe, resistant cases Surgical pophotectomy (removal of ovaries) considered as last resort

DIVERSITY AMONGST
WOMEN DIAGNOSED
WITH PMDD

Short Stories & Author Bio — Supplemental Section

SHORT STORIES

PMDD ruined my life before I even knew what it was. — by Steffanie Fuelkell

If I completely trusted our current modern healthcare system, I would assume women's health was well researched and funded. If I had stopped listening after what they told me, I wouldn't have survived this long. I was medically gaslit for ten years. After exhausting every option to stop the intense emotions, suicidal tendencies, and life-threatening depression, my medical team gave up. What they wanted me to try wasn't working, so I was labelled "treatment resistant" instead of them putting their egos aside, considering that maybe it's something they didn't know about. Women's health was never considered. Hormones are never considered. My cycle was never considered.

This is a list of everything I have tried, all the help I sought over those ten years, and no one connected it to women's health:

- Over 30 different medications and/or combinations of medications
- 6 different long-term therapists with active participation
- 3 psychologists
- 2 psychiatrists
- 200+ hours of different group therapies
- A month-long day program at a mental institution
- Numerous 911 calls and emergency room visits for self-harm and suicidal thoughts

- Having transcranial magnetic stimulation against my head—basically zapping my brain cells for an hour every day... for three months. This procedure has been used to treat psychiatric conditions by sending magnetic pulses to stimulate certain brain regions, inducing electrical currents in the brain tissue. This procedure is considered "non-invasive", but having an electromagnetic coil strapped to your head can, indeed, feel invasive when someone is recovering from other traumas.

- Committed myself to a psych ward for three weeks

I tried everything I possibly could and put 110% into my healing. The final straw was surviving a violent sexual assault, resulting in having to rely on a walker, to FINALLY get the proper referral for the injury to a women's health specialist who took my current health situation seriously.

Before I met Dr. Alicia Long, my plan for the past two years has been to apply for MAID when my pets pass away. If I were denied, I'd do it myself. She did not gaslight me. She took this very seriously and immediately understood that more drastic actions were required because this is real and can affect your life negatively in unimaginable ways. I can't live a normal life. I've been fighting it so long that I am long-term exhausted now, in and out of the hospital consistently. No matter what I do, I cyclically fight extreme depression and suicidal ideation, and now, I'm making plans. I can't fight this and at the same time fight all the cruel judgment, arrogant assumptions, and disappointing misunderstandings from the people who are supposed to love and support you through everything. Instead, those people who are supposed to fight in my corner with me made me feel like a burden. A monster. The perfect scapegoat.

My dad told me, "Only God and his church could save you". While also telling me I'm "too sensitive, too weak, suck it up, I'm not trying hard enough, don't be a burden on your sister". He was so mean to me in the name of God that I hated myself. I had to cut him off, and when that happens, the child is always to blame. What did the parent do to make their child feel so unloved? He was my biggest heartbreak and biggest bully. My self-love and happiness skyrocketed the first year without him involved in my life.

My sister works at a women's health clinic. She advocates so strongly and passionately for her clients and friends with women's health disorders/issues. I no longer look up to her as a leader in women's health advocacy when I learned she doesn't take MY health concerns seriously and gaslights me regularly. She has told me I'm not the only one with strong emotions and to go back to the psych ward if I want to hurt myself. She shows no compassion for me, wanting to end my life. I told her my plans for suicide. She doesn't care that years ago her friend's sister committed suicide, and told me she wanted us to be closer. She's had a few friends end their lives. And again, no empathy for me. Why? I'm exaggerating, I'm unwell, I'm not serious.

Some people only choose to see the surface. The biological reaction we can't really control. Not the science, mind, and heart behind it that is screaming for acceptance and understanding. This isn't something where relationships can thrive if the other party doesn't put the required effort in. Learn as much as you can, go to support groups online, and talk to a therapist. If you truly love someone, that's not too much to ask.

Along with all this bullshit, I've survived rapes, date rape, and sex trafficking. I have conquered my CPTSD, and my BPD has been in remission for three years. Post-traumatic growth is real, the idea that going through trauma makes us stronger in the end because we went through something different, learned lessons and skills, and chose to heal, all while increasing our strength and knowledge base.

Family means nothing when you're disrespected, blamed, and constantly being told you're not good enough. Only those who truly get to know me can recognize, acknowledge, and admire my extreme strength and resilience in the face of struggle from every direction in life. I spent years healing and in therapy, working on myself to become extremely self-aware and emotionally mature. Some can't understand the concept of dialectics, two things being true at once, one not existing without the other. I can be emotionally mature AND be sensitive at the same time. But heaven forbid a woman cries a lot, shows any depth of emotion, or refuses to stay silent. Instead, she's immediately labelled unstable, hysterical. "She should go to the psych ward".

Sound familiar? Now that I know this isn't my fault, as I was programmed to believe, I refuse to let this world take my heart or my voice or try to suppress and silence me any longer. I will not stop fighting for basic rights to women's health care.

We feel and react so deeply, so strongly. That's our body sending us a message. If there wasn't some sort of tiny unalignment in the first place, there would be nothing to amplify. If something brings up an enormous amount of emotion, that's a signal that it's something we need to dial into and heal. We literally cannot ignore the signs as they debilitate our lives.

But something no one tells you is that this can be alchemized into a gift. The first step is learning to be okay with being misunderstood. I cry easily and feel deeply. But I also heal deep. Feel the good emotions more deeply. These intense emotions we experience can be alchemized into a passionate drive for purpose and expansion. One just needs to find the right combination of modern and holistic health approaches and find the right outlets for those emotions. Peer support. Music with meaning. Sing. Dance. Drum. Create art.

Exercise. Scream and shake it out. Rage yell lyrics that speak to your pain and soul. Write it out. Burn it. Break shit safely at a rage room. Make a haunted dollhouse of your pain.

I like comparing PMDD cycles to Persephone's cyclical descent into the underworld. Goddess of Spring, Queen of the Underworld. That is a duality of power, strength, and grace. When in spring, we are fertile. We create. We collect. We harvest in preparation for winter. But the cyclic descent into the Underworld of darkness represents the shadows and negative emotions we face. A chance to work through anything that needs healing. You must feel it to heal it. Bottling up these strong emotions makes for an explosion later.

Allow your body to release anything it needs to during winter, our luteal phase.

Shed what needs to be shed to have a more efficient spring. Holding it in may make other people more comfortable, but it's hurting us at the same time. Instead of trying to fight the Underworld, we integrate it. Plan around it. Prepare for it. Use it. Consider it a ritual of divine feminine power.

My psychological and physical ailments are very real, and they are not going anywhere. While I have the opportunity and time to advocate for myself and my future, I hope to inspire others to do the same. Your traumas, your pain, your fight... are real. Speak up for yourself and don't let anyone make you feel that you don't have a voice when it comes to your body. You live in it, you know it better than anyone.

Thanks!

Steffanie Fuelkell

Meet Erica Barnes

I am 42 years old and originally from Ohio, and I relocated to Florida in 2019, where I lived until my husband and I recently relocated to New York.

I have always been fairly healthy until a severe allergic reaction to the influenza vaccine in December 2018, I ended up in the ER that night with a resting pulse of 200 and ended up seeing a cardiologist about a week later where after extensive testing I was diagnosed with supra ventricular tachycardia (SVT) and was prescribed a beta blocker which I will have to remain on for the rest of my life. He attributed it to a reaction to one of the vaccine ingredients and advised me not to receive any type of vaccine in the future because we don't know which ingredient caused the reaction. I also developed new medication allergies/sensitivities starting about a month after the reaction, with the most severe being an anaphylactic reaction to contrast dye during a routine pelvic CT scan, which caused seizures affecting the left side of my body. All scans must now be performed without contrast dye unless necessary, and then they must be done in the hospital with anti-seizure drugs on standby. My cardiologist in Florida believes my adrenal glands were damaged as a result of the vaccine reaction, which caused the SVT and new medication sensitivities. He agreed that I should not receive any more vaccines and also no new medications unless under close observation, as we don't know if my body will react. I also have endometriosis, which was diagnosed via CT scan and ultrasound after my third false appendicitis scare in late 2018. The radiologist said it was very unusual to be detected via scans alone, and the severe right pelvic pain was caused by endometrial tissue/adhesions near my appendix. The symptoms have improved over the past few years, except for ovulation pain, which is not as severe as before, when appendicitis was suspected. My OB said it will continue to get better as I approach perimenopause. I was also diagnosed with CPTSD two years ago, stemming from childhood trauma, finding my mother's body after she passed in 2018, and from a verbally/emotionally abusive relationship that I endured for two years.

I wasn't officially diagnosed with PMDD until I found my OB in 2023; she stated it was one of the most severe cases she has come across. She prescribed Sprintec birth control to stop my periods, but it caused such severe side effects, such as low pulse/blood pressure and dizziness, that I had to stop taking it after 3 days. We later learned that it should not be given to women who are taking beta blockers because it can raise the levels in the bloodstream, thus causing drops in pulse/blood pressure. My only option is an oophorectomy, but I have yet to find a doctor who will even consider doing the procedure. My OB said I am a candidate for a hysterectomy due to endometriosis, but that will not alleviate the symptoms of PMDD, and more needs to be done to prove I have the disorder. She said just because all my tests are normal doesn't mean I don't have it, but it will make the diagnosis trickier. My vitamin D levels are low, but two years of taking supplements did not help, and my primary doctor in Florida was hesitant to prescribe a higher dose due to my having very little body fat and the levels in my bloodstream possibly becoming toxic due to not having enough fat to absorb it. All my hormone and vitamin levels, such as magnesium and ferritin, have been tested multiple times over the last two years, and all are within normal range. At the suggestion of my therapist, who also suffered from severe PMDD until having an oophorectomy, I also tried taking aloe vera juice, ginkgo biloba, ginseng, zinc, and magnesium, but none of them made a difference. My husband and I follow a strict keto diet and used to eat red meat almost daily, but due to other health reasons, we've cut back to a couple of times a month during my luteal phase, as it has been shown to help alleviate symptoms, but unfortunately, that hasn't helped either.

I am hopeful for some answers/options soon, as this is taking a toll on my mental health, and I am also very concerned about how it is taking a toll on my marriage. The symptoms keep getting worse, and the fights that this causes between me and my husband each month are getting more volatile, including me feeling like divorce might be best for both of us, but then I go right back to feeling good again when the symptoms finally alleviate temporarily. He says he will always love me unconditionally and in sickness/health, but I am struggling to still believe that each month and feel he does not love me like he did before we got married and up until just a few months ago. Recently, out of frustration, he called my moods/feelings ludicrous and said he no longer wants to talk about it until I finally see a doctor. He later apologized and said it just hurts him so much to see me suffering, but I feel even more alone now, which makes me further doubt if he still loves me despite my struggles. I typically only have one good week each month (usually starting on day 17 or 18) and no longer have the good second week that, up until 2 months ago, took place during ovulation. I also have been out of work since January and trying to find something here in New York has been a struggle even though I am applying for anything/everything I can, I feel my husband and his cousin (who graciously opened up her home to us rent-free) resent me more each day as a result especially due to my mood swings and feel I am not trying hard enough because they think I can walk into a business and start working that day just like they did years ago. I feel I have no support from anyone and feel as though no one understands except for my therapist and those whom I have connected with via online support groups. At the suggestions of those in the IAPMD group on Facebook as well as the PMDD forum on Reddit I am hoping to find a doctor here in New York who specializes in functional medicine and also an endocrinologist so further testing such as the DUTCH test and various hormone/vitamin tests can be done then see about any treatments as well as get referred to a new OB so the oophorectomy option can be explored. There is also a case study going on at Columbia University, and I am hoping I can be part of it, as it will give me access to the specialists I need. It has been a long struggle, but I am hopeful I will eventually find support/treatment, and I need to keep reminding myself to stay strong throughout all this.

Alexa Torkelson — My PMDD Story

Journey to knowing (2012–2017)

My darkest and most difficult chapters of life occurred between the ages of nineteen and twenty-four. During these years, I traveled overseas, endured loss, went through a painful breakup of almost an eight-year relationship, had new roommate scenarios, new relationship lessons, and lived out of pure exhaustion from undergraduate studies. One experience that is imprinted in my memory from age twenty took place on a study abroad trip in Northumberland, England. This event started my curiosity around what my body and mind were battling that I could no longer tame on my own.

One evening, while the group of students I was with went to dinner, I left to go for a walk and found a nearby river to sit by. I sat down underneath this giant tree towering over the river and started to cry. I cried so hard; it was as if I added to the river with an outpouring of stories that my body was holding for far too long. For a while, I tried to make sense of these moments by calling it "the other me". However, this feeling of turning into another person each month started to be clockwork, and the symptoms were more and more frequent with every passing month. I could not shrug off the feeling anymore, and I became very afraid of the experience.

After my study abroad trip, I dove into my studies to complete my undergraduate degree as quickly as I could. This definitely allowed me to dissociate and was a distraction from tending to the continued unknowns of my cycle. The fear, however, stuck around for a few years before I got an official diagnosis at age twenty-four due to a second self-harm attempt that made me realize what was happening within my body and brain was bigger than my abilities to 'cope' with it all alone. This episode happened shortly after starting my master's program. I was on a mission to obtain a high-achieving degree during these younger years, so having these episodes ramp up when I least expected them robbed me of my studies and later became a huge struggle.

"The other me" became a "monster within" that needed a name. That name, Premenstrual Dysphoric Disorder.

Fast Forward to 2023 — A Short Reflection

I turned thirty this past year, and up until recently, I was managing the "monster within" with a lot more compassion, understanding, and attention. Yes, I still had a few tough cycles over the years. Yes, I still have moments curled up on the bathroom floor with enough tears to fill the tub. What seems to be different this time around is my ability to navigate the emotions that would have previously drowned me with more insight. I can name my triggers and choose better outlets for self-regulation that allow me to surf the wild, unpredictable emotional waves. I owe this to educating myself through IAPMD, reading others' stories similar to mine on the PMDD warrior blog page, my God-sent therapist, and certain people in my life who have persisted in naming why I am meant to be here in the world, even when everything in me has said otherwise. I still do not understand why I have to undergo such a painful journey; however, I am finding more strengths with every year that goes by.

In my first article, I posted on The Official Blog of Me V. PMDD, I was twenty-six. From twenty-four to twenty- six, I gained enough tools to complete my master's program in Marriage and Family Therapy, managing enough symptoms to provide care for others. As I continued to grow with more knowledge, make discoveries on what supports women most, and piece together the wounds of my past, I rapidly felt called to type out the start of my story, which became One Warrior's Experiential Path. It was the act of writing during that time in my life that gave me the most comfort, while making sense of this complex diagnosis.

After publishing that article, I then found a therapist (the God-sent one^^) and re-organized the messy parts of my life to try and make peace with the darker, uglier sides of myself, while also maintaining certain hobbies that brought me a lot of joy. I was getting better at having stronger boundaries and assigning "emotional containers" in my self-care routine to plug into when certain days became too overbearing. I started to see my whole life as an art piece, and I had to get downright honest with what creating a different lifestyle meant for me. I learned over time that this means having days built into my cycle (specifically the luteal phase) where I can intentionally tend to my body, inviting a slower schedule that allows me to move through painful moments with more ease and opportunities for rest.

The Dangers of Denial

In the fall of 2024, before the holidays, I hit an extremely hard wall that brought on a lot of mental hardships and overwhelming physical pain. I went back to a certain sense of fear I thought I had overcome, and it sent me on a very unexpected spiral. I decided to re-read my article entry on the PMDD Warrior site to see what messages younger me could be reminded of now. The one line that spoke loudly was, "The impulsivity in these trial moments is what makes us at risk to our own selves." I initially thought, "Damn. Why is it STILL so hard to hop off the impulsivity train once it starts going??". I also thought, "what a fu**ing life to be navigating five years later...". Radically, I switched my mindset to pick out a more comforting line to know I am still capable of conquering this beast of a cycle. This line being, I am courageously choosing to love it. 'It' being "the monster within". I sat with this statement and said it several times in my head while taking elongated breaths. Even at my worst, I still close my eyes and envision a younger version of me hugging a giant, furious-looking monster. It allows me to know both parts of me are accepted. I know at my core, I am allowed to love the monster within. It does not define me.

One fact that has stood true over the last fourteen years of navigating the many symptoms that come with PMDD is grappling with the fact that this disorder still has to be a part of my lifestyle. Even after years of hard work, therapeutic support, alternative remedies, pain management plans, and whatever 'healthier outlet' that has been recommended, there are just going to be really hard days.

The Denial is real. For me I spent a couple of years at the end of my master's program denying any of it was real because of the immense pain and confusion this illness brought on, let alone trying to have loved ones or a partner try to understand it. It was and has been at times easier to mask things, so I could rise above some other life challenges without hitting rock bottom. However, the masking never lasts very long, and the lows got scary low.

My Last Low

Between Thanksgiving and Christmas of 2024, I had three straight months of what felt like hell on earth. I was uncontrollably crying, in physical pain, could not remember anything or concentrate well, struggled to get out of bed, and became mentally stuck in suicidal ideation. It was incredibly defeating, and I was exhausted from trying to stay on top of my self-care tools while trying to complete two thousand hours for my MFT license.

Luckily, I had a supervisor within my master's program at this time to point me in some new directions. The first was seeing an MD, who referred me to get another perspective on how to work with these downfalls.

The second is understanding the root cause of my joint pain. This is something no one ever explored with me over many years of going to MDs and trying to understand how to control these layered symptoms. I will never forget standing in the kitchen that fall, struggling to open a peanut butter jar and then collapsing on the floor crying because I could not recognize the body I was living in once again. I also never considered that in all the years of navigating this disorder, the joint pain would become worse in my late twenties. I found out this pain can be amplified by inflammation. Since I have understood how inflammation gets stored in the body, I have a little journal in my kitchen where I have written down foods, supplements, and juices that reduce certain symptoms when I have extreme flare-ups.

It was during this low season that I created an emergency pain plan with my MD and connected with a chiropractor who specializes in Hormone Replacement Therapy (HRT). Both collaborated with me on a more sustainable, tangible care routine that the present day is providing me with the most symptom relief in years of being tossed around by only ideas. Both medical professionals have taken my story and tears extremely seriously in a way no other clinicians have before. I discovered certain deficiencies in my body that provided more clarity on foods I should eat. I also learned my testosterone levels were abnormally low for someone my age, which has already been a step in a positive direction.

What I have learned

In the early years of trying to identify what lifestyle changes meant, it was more like putting a bunch of Band- Aids on one giant wound, hoping one or two solutions might stick. Birth control spiked my suicidal ideation, SSRIs made me very tired and zombie-like, and outside of medication that was an opioid, I decided to give up on them all. What frustrated me during these years was that two weeks out of every month, my mind was clear, and I was fully functioning just fine. It did not make sense to be on a medication long-term when I enjoyed the person I was, most of the month.

The greatest, most eye-opening discovery I made on this continued journey was that there are three different types of PMDD. I read this in Shalene Gupta's published book, The Cycle. Out of her three explanations, I have type two, which is considered a "half-life". This means that I experience symptoms within a full two-week time span in my luteal phase, often each month. I further discovered that there is a neurosteroid called Allopregnanolone produced in the brain, which is a core contributor to the adverse reactions women with PMDD undergo during their worst days. Gupta states, "women with PMDD have an allergic reaction to allopregnanolone, causing severe disconnect in neurotransmitters within the brain that help your body function, allowing you to stay calm and cool (13)". I personally believe this is mind-blowing research and truly honor the women in this field of study who are validating what is happening when a woman's brain becomes disconnected from her bodily experience. So, all those times, "of feeling out of control", I really was feeling a lost sense of self.

Being able to find new strengths repeatedly, while reclaiming the strengths I already have identified with, has become easier with time and practice in picking up where I leave off after days of not being able to function well. The ups and downs of this cycle are traumatic within themselves. It is maddening, grief-filled, inexplicable at times...with a lot of thoughts like, "I wish I could go back to the child that never had these symptoms or knew them at all". I am currently leaning into more mindfulness routines in the mornings and inviting play back into my life in a way that gives me subtle reminders I am still the "curious, happy, and adventurous kid" I once was. I find the best reminders are the simplest ones.

Hard Truths

Drinking became my medicine at the age of twenty, and then it became a huge problem later down the road. I never admitted this out loud until recently. The reality is, I have had to radically name what became crutches when I did not understand what my body and mind were undergoing. Now, my personal work is a lot of ownership and recognizing the vicious habits that started taking away from achieving larger life goals. PMDD interfered with many opportunities in the past, where doors opened and I was unable to pursue certain offers because of my lack of self-esteem and fear that my symptoms would prevent me from being 'successful'.

I am not living in fear anymore; however, I am bravely learning that the more honest I am each step of the way, the more willing I am to pick another route and try again. I am okay with past decisions because I have WAY more compassion for the younger versions of myself that were misguided and incapable of self-love. During the year 2023, I spent four mornings a week reading books on self-compassion and spirituality to try to redefine my experience in a way I could not dismiss anymore. I owe it to slow mornings, no distractions, lots of rest, and holding myself with genuine loving arms. I am my own mother.

Continued Therapeutic Insights 2025

After I continued work with my MD, who specializes in women's health, preventative medicine, and community health, I was informed that the symptoms attached to PMDD will change as you get older, and naturally, your cycle will be changing each decade that goes by; it is never the same. This made me realize I will have to keep meeting myself each time my body decides to morph and change. I was also guided to understand that our gut is our second brain and encouraged to explore ways to get rid of toxins in my body, especially held within my intestines. I believe my body is still trying to flush out toxins and re-heal itself in a way I have held it captive by making poor diet choices in the past, especially under the extreme stressors that came with completing my degree.

Another major area I know has contributed to my symptoms, however, I never tied it to my menstrual cycle, was past relational wounds. When I found more clarity on this with my therapist, I quickly recognized that sexually damaging pastimes were "the demonizing symptoms" that I deemed uncontrollable at times. I have denied several sexual relational experiences that kept me in a terrible mental fixation when symptoms like anger, rage, depression, insomnia, and feeling out of control worsened in my luteal phase. I grew up in a culture where if hard things happened, "you just pick up your bootstraps and keep going". This mindset turned into an awful recipe that kept me trapped and engrossed with many past regrettable and shameful memories.

This messaging, however, was truly a byproduct of my homelife. I taught myself to keep all my emotions at bay for the sake of not seeing others react around me. This started at three years old. I have vivid memories of witnessing a parent's triggers and their inability to cope with their own mental health struggles, so I told myself, "I should never share what I think or feel with anyone". I did not want to cause someone else more pain than what they were already going through. I chose peace over truth. This mindset then grew like a virus over the years, and I made myself very uncomfortable, so others could stay happy. Needless to say, my nervous system was and has been pulsating with constant rage, with nowhere to scream it all out for longer than I knew.

The wild part of PMDD is, "even if I did scream, it's as though my body wants me to still remember the pain". That is the worst part of this monstrous visitor. You can continue overcoming wounds and feel proud of yourself for moving on, and then one day you wake up and your brain wants you to remember all the months and times you could not.

I believe for myself and a lot of women battling this disorder, there is a lineage of intergenerational traumas that come with how these symptoms get exacerbated later on in life. It may not be heavily researched yet, but I know some people carry the women's pain within their ancestry more than others. I know I became a vessel for the untold stories of women in my lineage. It is because of this that I now use my voice with more conviction, so I can put into words what another has not found yet.

Accepting the Parts of my Brain that can't do their Job Alone

Acceptance is my best friend. I physically feel my body healing itself from sexual and emotional trauma through breath work, EMDR, and other therapies that have assisted me in becoming whole again. After six straight months of exercise, adjustments at the chiropractor, and hormone replacement therapy, I am having more consistent days. I do not believe my brain is capable of rewiring neuro-steroids on its own. I have had to accept several forms of support that were hard at first and are now non-negotiable. I am beyond grateful for those friends, colleagues, clinicians, and family members who have tried to understand and encourage me to keep finding support when I wanted to give up. I have a unique relationship with my body and brain now, which will continue to carry a lot of wisdom as I continue to age.

The Problem

With years of my own research and reading other women's stories, there is a 'quick fix' issue with this diagnosis. It saddens me that most of my doctor experiences in my teen years were met with brief conversations about my period and quickly shifted focus to 'eat more bananas, it'll help give you potassium, and all is well' conversations. Given the complexity in symptomology each woman experiences and then adding in the different types of PMDD a woman could have, I have found it extremely trying to wrap my head around how to target the direct issue, without fear and uncertainty overriding my ability to make empirically validated, clear decisions for myself. Because this is chemically based and at the same time happens within a specific phase of a woman's menstrual cycle, it makes sense why there has been controversy and misunderstandings on how to best support women.

There are still taboos and corrections to be made in this field of study. I personally believe the suggestions around "go to" medications online for this diagnosis are not completely accurate. We have a way to go with more data on the most helpful medications and education on birth control options that have more long-lasting relief without triggering worse suicidal ideation, libido complications, becoming numb/stoic, extreme weight fluctuations, or worse; medication dependent. My MD has been very cautious, thoughtful, and real about medications. She once stated, "Certain medications are a bitch to go on and take even longer to get off". Knowing this, I am okay with our current pain management plan and not trying to find a medication that I would rely on in a way that would only add more symptoms to my journey of healing in the future. I have more trust in my own ability to slow down and tend to my physical health more intuitively and intentionally.

I feel less alone as more women are sharing their stories and talking openly about their experiences. I hope that as a collective of voices, we have more information that leads to more long-term, sustainable solutions that women trust and believe in. This diagnosis is no easy undertaking. I have to imagine many women with us now, and those who have passed at one point dreamt of a day with fewer internal battles to be able to stand in a dream that does not have to be re-dreamt over and over again. I am a dreamer at heart and always have been. I think overall, this has been the one quality of mine that allows me to press on.

This fight is not over.

As our bodies heal, voices are heard, and inner resilience strengthens, may there be opportunities for restoration and reclaiming what has been lost.

Poem — by Alexa Torkelson

A wild woman is the health of all women.

Through each cycle, a woman can be more in tune and more in love with each part of herself.

There is a conscious new enlightenment that happens with each phase and within the body's voice.

Listen

To distract, numb, and fear, the body's cycle is to feed the monster hiding in its cave.

You have to be courageous enough to look clearly at what is in front of you, walk into the cave, and face every symptom of the monster's rage.

This monster has crawled out every month to stomp me in the ground.

Now, I must approach it first.

Run

Show it I am stronger, fearless, and worthy of taming what it made impossible.

To befriend you, inner wild beast, is to be running freely in the world as the wild woman I am She is here

Here to play Here to stay

And if she finds herself under the foot of a monster, she knows not to let it define her skin.

Under this ground I walk on is a root system of knowledge

In this entanglement of untold stories, I know how to burrow out into a new day's light.

A light so intense that my feet are blithe and my chest is opened up to the sky
Look up monster

I dare you to pull out your claws.

You will not bury her.

Watch Me fly

Alexa Torkelson's recommended Care Kit:

- **Vitamins-** Magnesium, zinc, B12, Vitamin D, Omega 3
- **Reducing Anxiety/stress-** GABA Calm, Ashwagandha, Marea Wellness Supplements, Mud Water (replacing caffeine), anti-inflammatory foods
- **Inter-changeable self-care outlets-**Breathwork, Acupuncture, Talk Therapy, chiropractor, long walks, twenty minutes of 'daily hit workouts', cold river plunges, detox baths, journaling, painting, meditation apps and snuggles with my dog
- **Dotera Products-** Serenity gels, Calming blend capsules, calming bath oil, breathe oil, Deep blue oil, and clary calm oil
- **Recommended Books-** The Cycle byShalene Gupta**,** Addicted to the Monkey Mind by JF Benoist, The Untethered Soul by Michael A. Singer, Women Who Run with the Wolves by Clarissa Pinkola Estes
- **Emergency Pain Plan-** Indomethacin and Naproxen for severe inflammatory episodes. Indomethacin to help bring my brain back to my body in past episodes of dissociation. (As needed)

PMDD CARE KIT
Tools for Managing Symptoms and Building Resilience
My Vitimans
MUD WATER
Magnes uni
B12
Vitamin D
Secenity
Breathe
Deep Blue
GABA Calm
Athwingsube
PMDD CARE KIT
DoTerra Oils
Indonettacin
Ways I Reduce Stress
MUD-CALM
Aitzirrli Inmunoló
The Cycle
THE Untethered Soul
WOMEN WHO RUN with the WOLVES
Emergency Pain Plan
Journal
Detox Bath
Meditation App
Meditation Piklonlac
This kit reflects my journey to balance and wellness, not medical ad-vice. Please consult your healthcare provider before changing routine.

References

Suicide does carry a **markedly elevated risk** of suicidality (thoughts, plans, attempts) and a **higher risk of death by suicide** than women without premenstrual disorders.

What good studies show about PMDD/PMDs

- **Large registry (Sweden, JAMA Netw Open 2024):** Women with clinically diagnosed premenstrual disorders had **~2× higher risk of death by suicide** vs matched controls **(HR 1.92; 95% CI 1.42–2.60).** Risk was even **higher if diagnosed before age 25** (HR 3.84). Overall mortality was not higher, but suicide mortality was. (PMC)

- **Systematic review & meta-analysis (2021):** PMDD associated with **~7× higher odds of suicide attempt** and **~4× higher odds of suicidal ideation** vs women without PMDD. (PMC)

- **Systematic review (2020):** Among women with PMDD, **lifetime suicidal ideation ~37–46%**; **suicide plans ~17–19%**; **attempts ~13–16%**—all significantly higher than in controls. (PMC)

How does that compare with other high-risk disorders?

- **Borderline Personality Disorder (BPD):** About **10%** die by suicide; **~70%** attempt at least once—among the highest suicide mortalities in psychiatry. (PMC, NewYorkPresbyterian)

- **Bipolar disorder:** Long-term studies estimate **~7–8%** absolute risk of suicide after first hospital contact. (JAMA Network)

- **Eating disorders (esp. anorexia nervosa):** Highest **overall mortality** of any psychiatric illness; suicide is a major contributor. Meta-analyses show very high standardized mortality ratios and substantial attempt rates (e.g., **AN-binge/purge ~44%** ever attempted). (JAMA Network, BioMed Central)

Bottom line

- PMDD/PMDs substantially **increase suicide risk** and demand **active screening and prevention**, especially in the **late luteal phase** when symptoms peak.
- However, **BPD, bipolar disorder, and anorexia nervosa** generally show **equal or higher suicide mortality** than PMDD.

If you're in crisis or worried about safety: Call or text 988 (U.S.) or go to the nearest emergency room.

Additional Resources:

Infographic Summary: Game Girls (2018) Documentary

TITLE: Game Girls

DIRECTOR: Alina Skrzeszewska

RELEASE: 2018

SETTING: Skid Row, Los Angeles

STYLE: Documentary + Performance Art

PREMIERE: Berlin International Film Festival (Berlinale)

Central Focus:

The lives of Black and LGBTQ+ women experiencing homelessness, incarceration, and trauma in Skid Row, as told through the story of Teri Rogers and her then partner, Tiahna Vince.

Key Social Issues Highlighted Criminal Justice Impact:

- Teri is a formerly incarcerated Black woman.
- The film explores barriers post-release: housing, employment, and mental health.
- Systemic cycles of poverty → crime → incarceration → homelessness.

Substance Use Disorder (SUD):

- Shown as a response to trauma, violence, and instability.
- Not demonized but contextualized with empathy.

- Highlights failures of punitive vs. rehabilitative approaches.

PMDD (Premenstrual Dysphoric Disorder):

- While not named, emotional volatility and trauma hint at conditions like PMDD.
- Reflects how women of color are often untreated/misdiagnosed.
- Mental health symptoms are shown in connection with poverty, gender, and race.

Empowerment Through Art

- Theatre workshops become a tool for storytelling and healing.
- Women act out personal trauma and joy, reclaiming narratives.
- Creates safe spaces for emotional expression and identity.

Why It Matters:

- Reveals intersecting struggles: gender, race, poverty, mental health, and queerness.
- Challenges stigma around addiction, incarceration, and mental illness.
- Advocates for compassion, community, and systemic change.

"Game Girls" is not just a documentary. It is a mirror held up to society's forgotten women — fierce, hurting, and surviving.

About the Film

Game Girls follows two Black women living in Skid Row — as they navigate love, trauma, and survival through a mix of documentary and therapeutic theater workshops.

Focus Themes

1. PMDD (Premenstrual Dysphoric Disorder)

Mental health and the cost of invisibility

- PMDD causes severe mood and emotional symptoms before menstruation.
- Often **undiagnosed in marginalized women** due to lack of access to care.
- In the film, emotional dysregulation and trauma symptoms in Teri and others mirror PMDD struggles.
- Highlights the **intersection of gender, race, and medical neglect**.

"No one ever listens when a Black woman says she's in pain."

2. Criminal Justice Impact

From prison cells to Skid Row tents

- Teri is **formerly incarcerated**, like many women in the film.
- Reflects the **prison-to-homelessness pipeline** fueled by systemic poverty.
- After prison, barriers to jobs, housing, and support remain.
- Women are often criminalized for acts tied to survival (e.g., drug use, sex work).

Disproportionate statistics:

- 86% of incarcerated women have a history of trauma.
- Black women are incarcerated at nearly 2x the rate of white women.

3. Substance Use Disorder (SUD)

Addiction is not weakness — it's survival

- Many women in Skid Row use drugs to **cope with trauma** and instability.
- The film treats SUD with compassion, not judgment.
- Emphasizes the **lack of trauma-informed care** in recovery systems.
- Addiction is often criminalized rather than treated, feeding the justice cycle.

"We don't need more cops. We need counselors."

- *Game Girls* is more than a film — it's a lens into **intersectional injustice**.
- PMDD, incarceration, and addiction aren't separate issues — they **intersect** in systems that fail women.
- Art and storytelling are powerful tools for **healing and visibility**.

Further Resources

- **PMDD Advocacy**: iapmd.org
- **Justice Reform**: The Sentencing Project, ACLU
- **Substance Use Support**: Harm Reduction Coalition, SAMHSA

"Every step supports PMDD awareness"

★★★★★ 9.6
Prototype Satisfaction rate

SUMMARY

EXPRESS PROTOTYPE

PMDD by Teri Rogers

PRODUCT: Ready-to-wear custom pair
STYLE: Contemporary Sock Runner
PRODUCTION: Made in Italy
CRAFT: 100% Custom crafted
SKU: FR-085-2135830

Step Into Purpose.

The *PMDD by Teri Rogers* custom-designed sneaker is more than a fashion statement—it's a movement. Handcrafted in Italy with premium quality, this contemporary sock runner symbolizes resilience, awareness, and change. A portion of every sale directly supports research and advocacy for **Premenstrual Dysphoric Disorder (PMDD)**, helping bring hope and healing to millions of women worldwide. When you wear these shoes, you don't just walk—you carry the message forward.

PMDD Safety Card (Front)

■ Calming Reminders:

- *This will pass—PMDD is cyclical*
- *Symptoms are hormonal, not who you are*
- *You are not alone—support is available*

■ Quick Coping Tools:

- *Breathe (4-7-8 method)*
- *Journal or track moods*
- *Warm bath / music / walk*
- *Grounding (5-4-3-2-1 senses)*

PMDD Safety Card (Back)

■ Crisis & Support Contacts:

- *988 (Suicide & Crisis Lifeline)*
- *Text HELLO to 741741*
- *Therapist: ________________*
- *Friend/Family: ____________*

Expected Outcomes (Year 1)

- 20% increase in SSI/SSDI approvals for women with PMDD.
- Reduction in ER visits and psychiatric holds.
- Greater housing stability and fewer evictions.
- Reduced recidivism among justice-impacted women.
- National recognition of Los Angeles County as a leader in women's mental health equity.

Supporting Data & Visuals

PMDD and Suicide Risk

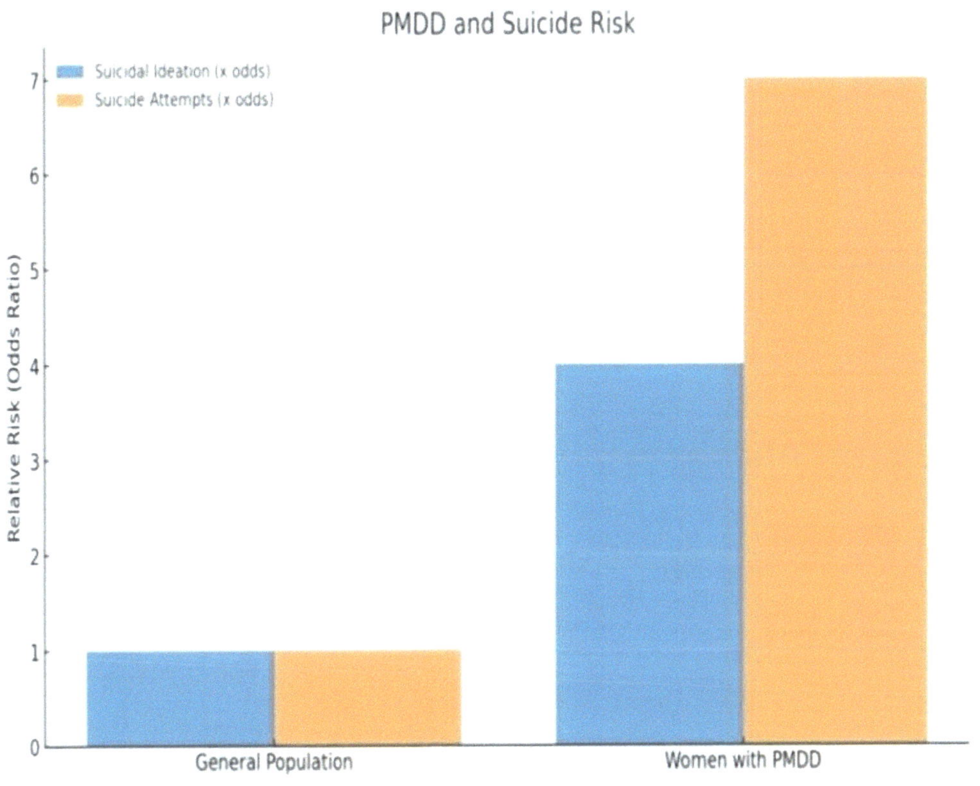

Pathway: PMDD Diagnosis to Housing Stability

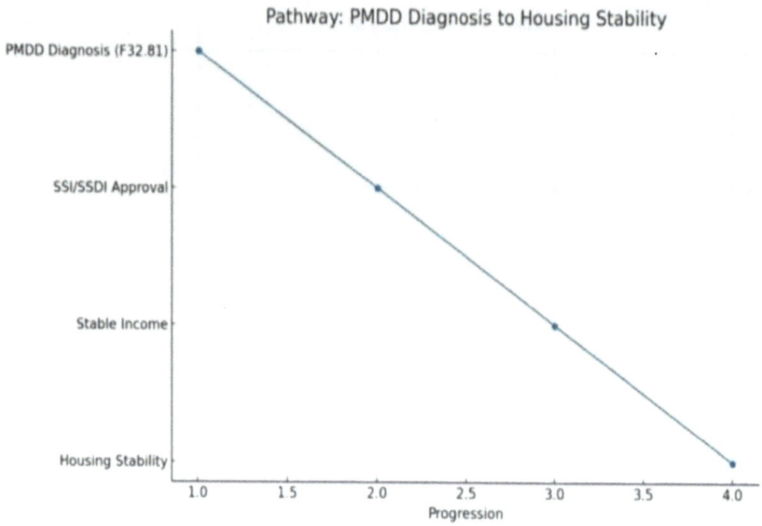

Estimated Cost per Crisis Episode

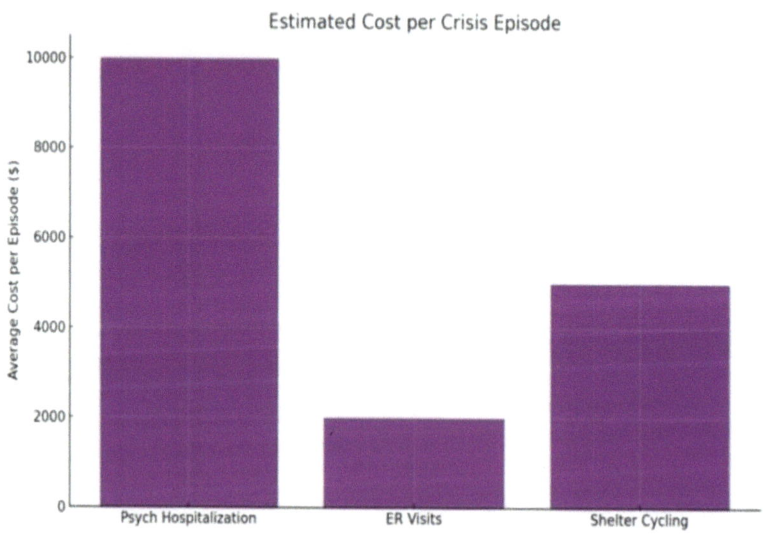

12-Month PMDD Advocacy Calendar

January
New Year, New Awareness
Tie-in: Goal-setting, mental health check-ins.
Action: Launch PMDD 101 webinar.

February
Reproductive & Hormonal Health
Tie-in: American Heart Month.
Action: Social posts on PMDD + hormones.

March
Endometriosis Awareness Month
Shared struggles with PMDD
Action: Collaborate with endometriosis orgs.

April
PMDD Awareness Month (Official)
Key Date: April 27 = Remembrance Day.
Action: Teal light-ups, panels.

May
Mental Health & Women's Health
Tie-ins: Mental Health Awareness, Women's Health W (M
Action: Run PMDD & MH campaign.

June
Mid-Year Check-In
Tie-in: PTSD Awareness Month.
Action: Publish coping strategies toolkit.

July
Uterine Fibroid Awareness Month (Purple)
+ Minority Mental Health Awareness Month (Green).
Action: Joint campaign on disparities.

August
Back-to-School & Family Wellness
Tie-in: National Wellness Month.
Action: Share resources for students.

September
Suicide Prevention Month.
Sept 10 – World Suicide Prevention Day
+ PCOS Awareness Month.
Action: Storytelling & crisis resources.

October
Mental Health Awareness Month
Oct 2 = Missouri PMDD Day
Oct 10 = World Mental Health Day.
Action: Partner with orgs.

November
Gratitude & Advocacy
Tie-in: Family Caregiver Month.
Action: Share caregiver perspectives.

December
Reflection & Hope
Tie-in: Holiday stress.
Action: Year-in-review; prep for April.

PMDD Symptoms: Physical, Emotional, and Behavioral

Premenstrual Dysphoric Disorder (PMDD) is a severe form of PMS with symptoms that disrupt daily life. Below is a detailed categorization of symptoms.

Category	Symptoms
Emotional / Psychological	• Depressed mood, hopelessness, worthlessness • Anxiety, tension, feeling 'on edge' • Mood swings, rejection sensitivity • Irritability or anger • Decreased interest in usual activities • Feeling overwhelmed or out of control • Cognitive difficulties: poor concentration, forgetfulness • Suicidal thoughts or self-harm ideation (severe cases)
Physical	• Bloating and water retention • Breast tenderness or swelling • Headaches or migraines • Joint or muscle pain • Severe cramps or pelvic pain • Gastrointestinal upset (nausea, constipation, diarrhea) • Appetite changes (cravings or reduced appetite) • Sleep disturbances (insomnia or hypersomnia) • Fatigue, low energy, sluggishness • Hot flashes or night sweats • Dizziness or lightheadedness
Behavioral / Social	• Social withdrawal and isolation • Impaired work or school performance • Conflict in relationships • Loss of interest in sex (low libido) • Increased substance use (alcohol, smoking, overeating) • Impulsive or risky behaviors

About the Author

Teri Rushawn Rogers is an award-winning author, speaker, and advocate whose life is a testament to resilience and redemption. Her memoir, *America's Game Girl: Bridging the Gaps – A Journey of Love, Mental Health, and Overcoming Stigma*, earned the International Impact Book Award in Addiction and Recovery and is distributed in every U.S. prison. She also appeared in the two-time award-winning documentary *Game Girls*, which brought her story to the screen. Teri is the Founder and CEO of Breaking Stigmas Treatment Operation, a 501(c)(3) nonprofit honored for its human and civil rights work. Today, she is dedicated to bringing urgent awareness to Premenstrual Dysphoric Disorder (PMDD), turning personal struggle into a mission of hope, healing, and change.

www.ingramcontent.com/pod-product-compliance
Lightning Source LLC
LaVergne TN
LVHW071239210926
848486LV00007B/302
* 9 7 9 8 2 1 8 7 8 1 9 1 0 *